WITHDR

SECRECY AND PUBLICITY

BY FRANCIS E. ROURKE

Intergovernmental Relations in Employment Security (1952)

With Malcolm Moos, *The Campus and the State* (1959)

Secrecy and Publicity: Dilemmas of Democracy (1961)

SECRECY

AND PUBLICITY

Dilemmas of Democracy

Francis E. Rourke

The Johns Hopkins Press
Baltimore

© 1961, THE JOHNS HOPKINS PRESS, BALTIMORE 18, MARYLAND

Distributed in Great Britain by Oxford University Press, London
Manufactured in the United States of America

Library of Congress Catalog Card Number 61-10736

FOR MEG

FOREWORD

THIS IS A study of the power that has come to rest in the hands of government officials to control a process vital to the health of modern democracy—the flow of information to the public.

The exercise of this power is felt throughout the length and breadth of government today. But its impact is sharpest in the areas of defense and foreign affairs, where public officials come closest to having monopoly power in the field of information, and where—through the skillful use of secrecy and publicity—they can wield an influence over public opinion not altogether different from that enjoyed by the autocrats of modern totalitarianism.

Indeed it is no exaggeration to say that the possibility of controlling communications has now opened up an avenue through which the gap between totalitarian and democratic government can progressively be narrowed, as modern dictators gradually substitute persuasion for coercion, and as democratic leaders acquire the ability to manufacture the consent upon which their authority is supposed to rest.

The point of view presented here is thus quite different from that to be found in such places as Walter Lippmann's recent book *The Public Philosophy*. For Lippmann, the principal peril to modern democracy lies in the fact that public opinion has assumed so great an influence over the decisions of democratic leaders that it threatens to devitalize the governing process. As Lippmann puts it with his characteristic eloquence:

> The people have imposed a veto upon the judgments of informed and responsible officials. They have compelled the governments, which usually knew what would have been wiser, or was necessary or was more expedient, to be too late with too little, or too long with too much, too pacifist in peace and too bellicose in war, too neutralist or appeasing in negotiation or too intransigent. Mass opinion has acquired mounting power in this century. It has shown itself to be a dangerous master of decisions when the stakes are life and death.[1]

Certainly it is no discredit to Lippmann, nor any disparagement to the pre-eminent position he has occupied in the study of public opinion for almost half a century, to point out that a danger of equal gravity to democracy looms on the landscape of modern politics from precisely the opposite direction —the possibility that public opinion may become all too submissive or inadequately critical of the follies and fallacies by which it is often led. Lippmann himself, in his discerning comments on the day-to-day conduct of foreign affairs, has had frequent occasion for concern over the servile posture of public opinion in contemporary democracy.

A word should also be said about the scope of this book. No study of the many-sided relationship between government and public opinion can claim to be exhaustive, and this inquiry into secrecy and publicity makes no such pretense.

For one thing, it is mainly confined to the experience of American democracy—an experience that has been heavily

---

[1] Walter Lippmann, *The Public Philosophy* (Mentor Edition, 1955), p. 24.

colored by certain unique characteristics of this society, including its passion for publicity and the weakness of traditions which would sustain the conventions of governmental privacy that are common in the democracies of western Europe.[2]

Moreover, the central focus of this book is upon practices which prevail in national rather than state and local government. To be sure, governmental communications present many similar problems at all levels of our federal system. But there are differences also, most notably perhaps, the fact that state and local officials have nowhere near the power to influence public opinion on matters under their jurisdiction that national officials have in an area like atomic energy.

Many persons at The Johns Hopkins University have been of great assistance to me in completing this study, and I would like to express my appreciation to them. My colleagues and graduate students in the political science department have all given me the benefit of advice on matters on which their knowledge is greater than my own. I owe a special debt of gratitude to Professor Robert W. Tucker, who read the original manuscript in its entirety and made many suggestions for its improvement.

For their help at various points in bringing this manuscript to publication, I would also like to thank Beatrice Blakslee, documents librarian, and Edna Fulton, secretary of the political science department at the university.

This manuscript was completed with the help of a grant from the Public Affairs Committee established at The Johns Hopkins University under the auspices of the Ford Founda-

---

[2] See in this regard Brian Chapman, *The Profession of Government* (N.Y., 1959), p. 321. As Chapman points out, secrecy in European bureaucracy "dates from the time when government business was the concern of the monarch himself, or of a very small group of political and administrative leaders convinced that they were innately more intelligent, better bred and more profoundly patriotic than the rest of the population."

tion, and I am grateful to both the committee and the foundation for their generous aid.

I would also like to thank the publishers of the University of *Chicago Law Review*, the *Political Science Quarterly*, and the *American Political Science Review* for permission to reprint materials which originally appeared in these journals.

FRANCIS E. ROURKE

Baltimore, Maryland
February 15, 1961

TABLE OF CONTENTS

". . . the old rationalist assumptions of Locke and of liberal democracy have broken down under the weight both of changed material conditions and of new scientific insights and inventions, and the leaders of the new democracy are concerned no longer primarily with the reflexion of opinion, but with the moulding and manipulation of opinion."

E. H. Carr, *The New Society* (1951)

CHAPTER 1

GOVERNMENT AND PUBLIC OPINION

ONE OF THE truly singular characteristics of modern society is the extraordinary interest all governments now manifest in the shape of public opinion. In the case of modern democratic states this concern is noteworthy more for the intensity it has assumed than for the fact of its existence, since democracy has always rested—in philosophical assumption if not in practical fact—upon the support of public opinion. Even so, however, there is no question but that over the past century the role of public opinion in the operations of democratic states has come to assume increasing importance—with the growth of population, the elimination of suffrage restrictions, the organization of political parties and pressure groups, and the emergence of a milieu in which politicians find it increasingly expedient to cater to the tastes and preferences of the masses.

What is infinitely more striking is the passion modern despotism has now acquired for the art of public relations, for nothing more clearly separates modern from traditional authoritarian government than the stress contemporary dictatorship puts upon arousing and maintaining public support, even though technological development has long since given it instruments for putting down opposition by force immensely superior to anything the monarchs of old ever enjoyed. But the plain fact of the matter is that the new-style despotism depends upon public enthusiasm for its policies, both domestic and foreign, because these policies so often require co-operation or even sacrifices on the part of the citizen for their success. No five-year plan can achieve its goals in the face of public lethargy.

A principal effect of this heightened governmental interest in the character of public opinion is a heavy involvement by the state in the process by which the community forms its opinions. As far as dictatorships are concerned, this commitment is indispensable to the maintenance of authoritarian control. The ministry of information is a focal point of ideological indoctrination for believers, as well as for verbal assault upon heresies that may threaten to spring up. The management of public opinion is no less critical an attribute of the modern totalitarian state than central direction and control of the economy. As one student of Soviet affairs has noted: "the state establishes for the media specific, concrete, and practical goals, which are treated much like the production norms set for Soviet industry." [1]

In the case of modern democratic states, the role of government in the communications process is necessarily more circumscribed. The existence of a free press and broadcasting industry would alone tend to insure this result, since these media are understandably jealous of governmental competition in their efforts to report current events. But even in a democracy, the influence of government upon the process of opinion formation is nonetheless very great, since the operations of the private media of communications are subject to some degree of influence by public agencies, and government itself is the source of much of the information upon which the

---

[1] Alex Inkeles, *Public Opinion in Soviet Russia* (Cambridge, Mass., 1950), p. 318.

community's political opinions are ultimately based. There are those who argue that the influence that democratic government has today come to exert over the communications process, particularly in the area of foreign affairs, has given it possibilities for manipulating public opinion not altogether different from those enjoyed by communist regimes on the other side of the Iron Curtain.

These possibilities were given dramatic emphasis by the events surrounding the U-2 affair—the ill-fated flight of an American reconnaissance plane over the Soviet Union on May 1, 1960. The fact that such a plane had been shot down was first announced by Premier Khrushchev on May 5, 1960. For two days following this announcement, the American government stoutly insisted that the aircraft was a weather observation plane which had accidentally blundered over the Turkish-Soviet border when the pilot's oxygen supply gave out. The U. S. National Aeronautics and Space Administration issued an elaborate account of the scientific investigations being carried on through high-altitude observation; and leading newspapers, such as the *New York Times*, were moved to editorial ridicule of Soviet concern over "an accidental violation of Russian air rights." [2]

Then on May 7, 1960, Khrushchev sprang his trap: the plane had been shot down twelve-hundred miles past the border of the Soviet Union; the pilot had been captured; and he had confessed to being an employee of the Central Intelligence Agency sent aloft on the mission of photographing Soviet military installations. At this point the Eisenhower administration was forced into a rapid about-face. It confirmed and eventually defended the fact that the U-2 had been on an intelligence mission. After the subsequent break-up of the summit conference, President Eisenhower explained that the false account of the U-2 incident originally issued by the government

[2] *New York Times*, May 7, 1960, p. 22.

represented "what is known in intelligence circles as a covering statement," designed to protect our intelligence operations from being disclosed to the enemy.

The implications of this event for American democracy are as yet not altogether clear. Insofar as a reaction was visible, the public did not seem greatly disturbed by this official effort to conceal the facts with "covering statements" when it proved expedient to do so. But the original fabrication was followed so quickly by a true account, and so many other events were coupled in the public mind with the release of false information, including Premier Khrushchev's violent personal attacks upon President Eisenhower, that it is difficult to identify the precise public response to that part of the U-2 affair which involved the deliberate misrepresentation of facts by high government officials. It is too early to say that the public is prepared to give unqualified acceptance to governmental falsehoods as long as they seem to serve the security interests of the United States, but the U-2 affair certainly presents the possibility that this is now the case.

In any event, the incident provides a clear indication of the power that has come to rest in the hands of government officials to influence public attitudes in foreign affairs through their control over the release of information by which these attitudes are partially formed. For some forty-eight hours at least, American public opinion on the U-2 affair was shaped by information at variance with the facts—information that responsible officials knew to be false when it was released. While cases in which such deception occurs may be the exception rather than the rule in any healthy democracy, the possibility of their occurrence has been heightened by the increased importance of military and diplomatic affairs—areas in which it is difficult to obtain access to the facts except through official channels, and where official activities themselves are often shrouded in secrecy.

Some Historical Precedents

Concern over the impact of government upon public opinion is by no means a new phenomenon in American politics. It found expression very early in the history of this country in the inclusion in early state constitutions, as well as in the national Constitution, of strict guarantees of freedom of speech and of the press. These guarantees reflected a strong determination that the power of government should never be used to impede the free expression and exchange of private opinion within the community. And by and large, they have stood the test of time very well, although subject to some attrition during periods of war or nationalist fervor. In this country it has been largely the pressure of community opinion, rather than government control, that has served to discourage the free expression of unorthodox views.

But it was also recognized at a very early date that while government should not impede, it could do a great deal to facilitate the process of communications within society. When the Post Office and the system of post roads were first established, one of their primary functions was that of improving the community's ability to inform itself. The dissemination of accurate information among the citizens on public affairs had implications for some statesmen that were as much political as they were educational, for it was believed that people in isolated areas could be misled into sedition or insurrection only if they were prevented by poor communications from obtaining access to the truth.[3]

But the fact that such an instrument of education could also

[3] For information on early activities by government agencies affecting the communications process, see Leonard D. White, *The Federalists* (New York, 1948), and *The Jeffersonians* (New York, 1951).

serve as a vehicle for influencing political belief did not escape attention. In 1790, for example, a Federalist proposal to give the president the right to determine where post offices and post roads should be located was bitterly opposed in Congress on the grounds that it would give the chief executive extraordinary power over the shape of public opinion. As one critic put it: "If the post office were to be regulated by the will of a single person, the dissemination of intelligence might be impeded, and the people kept entirely in the dark with respect to the transactions of Government." [4]

Shortly thereafter, the Federalists themselves gave a similar reason for opposing Jefferson's suggestion that Tom Paine be appointed postmaster general. In the Federalist view, such an appointment would give Paine an unparalleled opportunity to stir up discontent: "Should he [i.e., Paine] be intrusted with the patronage of the Post Office department, pervading the whole country, this channel for the dissemination of insurrectionary opinions would be entirely under Jefferson's command; for, both as to politics and religion, Paine and Jefferson had similar views." [5] During his presidency, Jefferson himself later extended the system of post roads on the grounds that it is "a matter of the highest importance to furnish the citizens with full and correct information." [6]

There were other areas in which government information activity assumed early importance. Executive reports to Congress provided much of the information on which legislative decisions were based during this period. The influence that the reports and proposals of Alexander Hamilton exerted while he was serving as Secretary of the Treasury has become legendary, but executive influence over legislative action was not restricted to his tenure of office. In summing up the careers

[4] White, *The Federalists*, p. 79.
[5] *Ibid.*, p. 225, footnote 12.
[6] White, *The Jeffersonians*, p. 299.

of the Jeffersonian presidents who succeeded to power after Hamilton's retirement, Leonard White has noted that,

> Substantially all major legislation and much minor legislation were based on administrative reports, giving facts and opinions for the guidance of Congress . . . requests for facts represented a normal part of the interplay between Congress and the executive departments. The latter acted in this respect somewhat in the capacity of staff aides to committees of Congress, none of which had any assistance of their own.[7]

This period also saw the first use of governmental publicity for punitive purposes. Even though it led to some embarrassment for executive officials, Congress at this time inaugurated the practice of publicizing all unsettled accounts in the executive branch, a requirement which revealed that two of the chief accounts on which books had not yet been closed were with ex-Presidents John Adams and James Monroe. Jefferson also insisted upon disclosing the salaries of all executive officials, on the grounds that this publicity would help check any undue expansion in the size of the executive branch.

This employment of the power of publicity as a deterrent to malpractice was one of the many ways in which contemporary issues in information policy were foreshadowed at the very beginning of our history, as the power of government over public opinion stirred widespread concern in the law and practice of early American politics. However, these apprehensions have been greatly magnified during this century, and particularly in the period since World War II. For the issues that have arisen on the contemporary scene stem in good part from the steady expansion in the scope of state activity that has occurred during recent decades—a development that has opened up avenues for governmental influence over public opinion that could scarcely have been anticipated when this nation was first established.

[7] *Ibid.*, pp. 93–94.

The Range of Contemporary Issues

Today, for example, it is widely believed that government secrecy has now reached the point where it so seriously constricts the availability of information about public affairs as to threaten the vitality of democracy itself, or at least the opportunity for informed discussion that is the essence of free government. J. Russell Wiggins, Managing Editor of the *Washington Post*, is one of the stoutest advocates of this point of view:

> The more that government becomes secret, the less it remains free. To diminish the people's information about government is to diminish the people's participation in government. . . . The arguments for more secrecy may be good arguments which, in a world that is menaced by Communist imperialism, we cannot altogether refute. They are, nevertheless, arguments for less freedom.[8]

As Wiggins indicates, the growth of secrecy within present-day American government reflects in large measure the presence of international tensions. In this respect as in many others, the current development of American life has taken its cue from the force of Soviet pressure. In the missile race, for example, the advantages of secrecy as a tactical asset have been increasingly underlined by emerging events. It is the means by which the Soviets have concealed their plans, hidden their blunders, and prevented comparisons unfavorable to them. The U-2 affair provides a compelling indication of the length to which we will go to overcome Soviet secrecy, even risking, as in this case, the initiation of a chain of events that might end in thermonuclear war.

To be sure, the development of secrecy in American gov-

[8] James R. Wiggins, *Freedom or Secrecy* (New York, 1956), p. ix.

ernment had its origins long before the first satellite was put into orbit or before Khrushchev or Marx himself was actually born. Even apart from military matters, presidents and other high executive officials have always argued that a certain measure of privacy is essential for the effective conduct of civilian affairs, principally on the grounds that it invigorates executive deliberations by protecting career officials from political reprisal for incautious remarks or proposals they may offer. This is the foundation upon which has been erected a doctrine of "executive privilege"—the notion that executive officials have an inherent right to withhold information from the public and the legislature. But down through the years, this effort to preserve a degree of privacy in the conduct of executive activities has stirred repeated conflict, and on more than one occasion has triggered a major crisis in the relations between president and Congress.

What is distinctive about governmental secrecy today is the vast range of information that is now subject to laws prohibiting the disclosure of official data. Apart from the classification system in national defense, which attempts to conceal a wide variety of military and diplomatic secrets from foreign espionage, there have been a great number of statutes enacted and executive regulations promulgated which attempt to prevent the unauthorized release of non-defense but nevertheless confidential information. And in areas where secrecy is not sanctioned by such specific legal safeguards, presidents can always invoke their executive privilege to withhold information when they choose to do so. As a result there is virtually no area of the administrative process that has been left untouched by the claims of secrecy in modern American government.

The difficulties that governmental secrecy present in contemporary American politics have been enormously complicated by the fact that they coexist with and are related to a formidable range of questions that have been raised by the growing role of government in the field of publicity. This problem looms largest in the field of military and diplomatic affairs, as has already been noted in discussing the U-2 incident, where a deliberate attempt was made to mislead world opinion through the release of false information. But from the beginning of this century, Congress has been highly alarmed by the role of informational activity in the work of all executive agencies. These apprehensions over administrative press agentry have swelled rather than receded with time, as new instruments of persuasion have been added to the weaponry of government public relations. The advent of radio and television and the growing orientation of the entire community around national affairs has now brought brain-washing on a nationwide scale within the range of at least technical possibility.

But the manipulation of official information to control community opinion is by no means the only danger that governmental use of publicity today presents. For it has become increasingly clear that the weapon of publicity can be used not only for the purpose of engineering consent on the part of the community, but also to punish individuals when the government chooses to do so. Publicity as a punitive sanction has come to be recognized as a serious problem only in comparatively recent times, with the vast expansion that has occurred in government regulatory activity and the extension of congressional investigations from governmental affairs into areas of social and economic activity outside of government itself. During recent years, congressional inquiries into subversion, gambling, drug prices, television quiz shows, and a host of other subjects have brought home the fact that the power of publicity can be used with telling effect not only against government officials but also against obscure as well as highly placed private citizens. The anguish of innocent parties in-

jured by the publicity connected with congressional hearings
has inspired a great deal of the zeal for reforming the investigative process that has been visible during recent years.

The cutting edge of publicity in the field of administrative
regulation is reflected by the ability of agencies such as the
Securities and Exchange Commission and the Food and Drug
Administration to secure compliance with the statutes they
administer through the mere threat to publicize evidence of illegal activity that they uncover in the course of their investigations. Other regulatory agencies have used this technique
of control through exposure with similar effect. For example,
the fair-employment agencies that now exist in several of the
states have found that fear of unpleasant publicity plays a
very important role in bringing about the enforcement of anti-
discrimination laws.

The power of publicity as a technique of governmental coercion has presented perplexing problems of civil liberties, insofar as its use is not hedged about with the same restraints
as are attached to such traditional legal sanctions as fines or
imprisonment. The damage the cranberry industry suffered in
1959 as a result of an official statement released by the Food
and Drug Administration just before Thanksgiving warning
the public against the purchase of contaminated berries provided a clear indication of both the effectiveness of official
publicity as a technique of control and the adverse effect
publicity may have upon those against whom it is used.

In 1960, Protestant clergymen associated with the National
Council of Churches of Christ were also exposed to the punitive side of government publicity as a result of the publication
of an Air Force training manual linking the Council (as well as
Protestant churches generally) with communism. Although
the Secretary of the Air Force subsequently ordered the manual withdrawn from circulation, he did so "without any determination as to whether the charges were true or false." Indeed

the council never was able to obtain a satisfactory retraction from the government, in spite of the fact that publication of these charges by an official agency was, in the Council's view, "a patent violation of the free exercise of religion as guaranteed by the First Amendment to the Constitution of the United States." [9]

But while official use of publicity often results in injury to private citizens, the fact remains that government information activities can serve the health and welfare of the community in an infinite variety of ways. It is necessary only to cite the educational program carried on by the Social Security Administration to inform beneficiaries of the old-age and survivors insurance system of their pension rights, or the efforts of local public health authorities to convince residents of their communities to avail themselves of the Salk vaccine against polio outbreaks, or the never-ending, if none too fruitful, attempts of highway commissions to cut down the number of motor vehicle accidents through widely publicized safety campaigns. The truth of the matter is that publicity, like science, is the Promethean gift with which modern government has been both blessed and cursed.

Publicity, Secrecy, and Democracy

If there is a single assumption underlying this book, it is the belief that no aspect of the subject of government information activity can be dealt with adequately except in conjunction with the whole range of problems presented by publicity and secrecy in government. Criticism of governmental secrecy, for example, cannot ignore the role that restrictions upon the release of official information may play in protecting private individuals against needless damage from adverse publicity.

[9] *New York Times,* February 25, 1960, p. 13.

This is not to suggest that measures intended to shield private persons from unfavorable attention are always immune from criticism even if they result in a serious reduction in the availability of information about public affairs. It is only to point out that the need for disclosure is not the sole yardstick by which government information activity can be appraised.

Similarly, concern over government publicity needs to focus not only upon the dangers of an official propaganda machine, but also upon the fact that there are respects in which the public interest can easily suffer more from the weakness than it does from the strength of government publicity. This may be a special problem in the case of activities such as civil defense and water pollution control—programs that have high priority in terms of community welfare but low standing as far as public interest is concerned. Thus, no study of government information activity is complete if it entirely neglects the possibility that in some areas we may suffer not from "brainwashing" but from the inability of government to gain the attention of the community.

It would not, perhaps, be necessary to make these observations were it not for the fact that public discussion of government information activity is so largely shaped by journalists and others connected with the communications media. As a result, there has been a tendency to place great emphasis upon those aspects of the problem of information policy which threaten the valid interests of the newspaper and television industry. These interests are challenged primarily by excessive publicity, which presents the spectre of governmental competition in reporting the news, and executive secrecy, which threatens to block off access to news. It has not always been as forcefully pointed out that the public interest may also suffer damage from ineffective publicity or insufficient privacy in the affairs of government.

Here as elsewhere in matters of public policy, the problem

is one of striking a balance. And in arriving at such a point of equilibrium in the field of government information practices, it is important to consider not only the claims that need to be weighed in the balance, such as the need to stimulate the maximum flow of information to the community and to prevent the disclosure of state secrets to a national adversary, but also the degree to which each of these conflicting interests is effectively represented in the process of pressure and counter-pressure through which public policy in a democracy is so largely hammered out.

It is in other words a matter of estimating the practical likelihood that any of the dangers with which we are confronted in the field of information activity may occur. There can be no doubt, for example, that there are vitally important issues of public policy where practices of governmental secrecy are carried so far as to seriously impede public scrutiny and appraisal of official performance. In the past these issues have included the adequacy of national defense, the practical limits and possibilities of disarmament, and the effectiveness of American foreign policy. Here the prestige and authority of military agencies weigh so heavily in the scales, or considerations of national self-interest appear to be so overriding, that resort to gross practices of secrecy may go unchallenged, while newsmen and legislators are bending every effort to force a more vulnerable civilian agency to disclose some petty detail on payroll information that it has been accused of withholding.

At the same time, however, there are other areas in which it has become increasingly difficult to prevent pressures for publicity from getting out of hand. "Exposure for exposure's sake," as the Supreme Court has noted, is by no means a political necessity in a free society, since the values of democracy permit and even encourage a large measure of privacy at the polling place, in the jury room, and elsewhere. And it may be far from prudent, in view of the substantial contribution privacy often makes to the efficiency of democratic government, not only in diplomacy but in domestic administration as well. There is no more difficult task facing the modern democratic state than that of containing pressures toward excessive publicity, without at the same time encouraging practices of secrecy which choke off the flow of information about public affairs upon which the vitality of government by discussion essentially depends. These are among the central problems that arise in reconciling the conflicting claims of publicity, secrecy, and democracy.

PART ONE

SECRECY IN AMERICAN BUREAUCRACY

CHAPTER 2

THE GROWTH OF SECRECY

MAX WEBER, in his classic analysis of bureaucracy as a form of social organization, holds that a preoccupation with secrecy is an inherent characteristic of administrative institutions.[1] According to Weber, this preoccupation is based in good part upon functional necessity. Government agencies, as well as organizations in the sphere of private bureaucracy, find it expedient to keep certain phases of their operations secret in the interest of maintaining a competitive advantage over rival administrative units. For governmental organizations this need is especially pronounced in the area of military and diplomatic operations. In any nation-state, military administration must, in Weber's words, "insist on the concealment of its most important measures."[2] The stake of private organizations in administrative secrecy is likewise high and stems from such factors as the possession of trade secrets which need to be kept safe from the espionage of business rivals.

However, while administrative secrecy has its roots in a perfectly rational concern on the part of an administrative organization for its efficiency or even its existence, Weber also

[1] H. H. Gerth and C. Wright Mills (eds.), *From Max Weber: Essays in Sociology* (New York, 1946), pp. 196–244.
[2] *Ibid.*, p. 233.

21

argues that this legitimate concern tends inevitably to transform itself into an obsession. The secrecy which begins as a means toward the achievement of organizational objectives becomes in time an end in itself. Weber's explanation of this development in the area of public administration is that it originates in a conscious desire on the part of bureaucracies to insulate themselves from effective outside control. "In facing a parliament," Weber writes, "the bureaucracy out of a sure power instinct, fights every attempt of the parliament to gain knowledge by means of its own experts or from interest groups." [3]

However, it is equally plausible to maintain—along lines traced in the work of Robert Merton,[4] among others—that it is in the nature of bureaucracy to transform procedures into purposes and that an obsession with secrecy is but a single manifestation of this general tendency. A rule requiring secrecy is established, with disclosure being authorized only in unusual cases, and the path of least resistance for the bureaucrat becomes that of following the general rule and avoiding recognition of disconcerting exceptions. Here is Dean Wigmore's view of the way things happen when an administrative agency is asked for information it regards as confidential:

> The subordinate at [the] lowest point, obsessed by the general dogma against disclosure, prepares a reply denying the application; he will usually not have the initiative or the courage to propose an exceptional use of discretion in favor of granting the application.[5]

The same point was made by a congressional committee which recently studied administrative secrecy: "In hearings

[3] *Ibid.*, pp. 233–34.

[4] Robert K. Merton, *Social Theory and Social Structure* (Glencoe, Illinois, 1949), pp. 153–55.

[5] John Henry Wigmore, *A Treatise on the Anglo-American System of Evidence in Trials at Common Law* (Boston, 1940), Vol. 8, p. 793.

with . . . departments and agencies, the subcommittee has found that laudable information programs are expressed by the top agency officials, but these programs often are not spelled out clearly for the guidance of the employees at the working level who release or restrict information." [6] If these appraisals are correct, an exaggerated tendency toward secrecy in administration can be traced as much to bureaucratic inertia or timidity as to what Weber regarded as a lust for power.

The American Tradition of Publicity

American administration, it has often been noted, fails in many respects to conform to the stereotype of bureaucracy as presented in Weber's analysis.[7] For one thing, the bureaucratic role has traditionally been less professionalized in American society than has been the case in Europe. The idea of a career bureaucracy through which individuals would give their lives to the service of the state has had difficulty establishing itself in this country. For this reason, and because of the wealth of economic opportunities available in the private sector of the community, there has been a constant movement to and from the ranks of bureaucracy by patronage and other short-term employees.

This ease of entrance and exit from bureaucracy has handicapped the development of a high degree of secrecy in administrative operations. In office, the short-term employee has less time to become habituated to acceptance of institutional rules governing his official behavior, regulations that may, for example, require the withholding of information acquired in the line of duty. Out of office, such employees provide a fruit-

[6] *Second Report by the Committee on Government Operations,* 85 Cong., 1st Sess., House Report No. 157, Feb. 22, 1957, p. 46.
[7] See, for example, Dwaine Marvick, *Career Perspectives in a Bureaucratic Setting* (Ann Arbor, 1954), pp. 1–4.

ful source of information regarding the internal affairs of bureaucracy, and congressional hearings and other forums from which they may display this knowledge are not lacking.

Apart from these conditions peculiar to American bureaucracy itself, other factors in the general environment of American politics militate against the development of secrecy in administration. Not the least of these is what has been called the tradition of "luxuriating publicity" in American democracy.[8] The American view has traditionally been that the operations of government no less than other areas of life should be subjected to continuous scrutiny through the searching spotlight of publicity. The premise upon which this view rests is that nefarious activities on the part of government officials can be prevented in no better way than by fear of exposure before the bar of public opinion. Compared to publicity, such internal checks upon bureaucratic misbehavior as a code of honor or of professional ethics are considered to have but negligible value.

Distaste for government secrecy has found repeated expression in the development of American political thought. Very early in our history it was enunciated in the words of Edward Livingston: "no nation ever yet found any inconvenience from too close an inspection into the conduct of its officers; but many have been brought to ruin and reduced to slavery, by suffering gradual imposition and abuses, which were imperceptible, only because the means of publicity had not been secured." [9] It was, however, in the Progressive era, around the beginning of this century, that the attack on secrecy reached its peak and found its most eloquent spokesman in the person of Woodrow Wilson:

[8] Edward A. Shils, *The Torment of Secrecy* (Glencoe, Illinois, 1956), pp. 37–44.

[9] *The Complete Works of Edward Livingston on Criminal Jurisprudence* (N.Y., 1873), Vol. I, p. 15. This passage was first published in 1822.

I, for one, have the conviction that government ought to be
all outside and no inside. I, for my part, believe that there ought
to be no place where anything can be done that everybody does
not know about. . . . Everybody knows that corruption thrives
in secret places, and avoids public places, and we believe it a fair
presumption that secrecy means impropriety. . . . Government must, if it is to be pure and correct in its processes, be absolutely public in everything that affects it.[10]

The "open covenants openly arrived at" provision subsequently included in the Fourteen Points was merely an application to international affairs of a principle that Wilson believed to be deeply rooted in the inner logic of democracy.
(Most other observers, however, have placed far greater stress
upon the importance of privacy in facilitating diplomatic
negotiations.)

A varied set of institutions have helped to maintain the
vitality of this tradition of disclosure in American administration. At all levels of government, legislatures and, in particular, legislative committees have been insistent that the affairs
of administration should be open to their own and at the same
time to public inspection. In holding to this position, legislatures have been inspired by the belief that the legislative task
demands access to all information in the hands of executive
officials. While representative bodies have not always been
successful in enforcing their claim, the pressure they have exerted in this direction has had an important effect in holding
administrative secrecy within much narrower limits than would
otherwise be the case in American government.

By comparison, European legislatures have been much less
successful in compelling disclosure by executive agencies of
the affairs of state. It has been pointed out, for example, that
civil servants in the United Kingdom enjoy much more ex-

[10] *The New Freedom* (New York, 1913), pp. 92–104.

tensive privileges of secrecy than is the case in the United States.[11] And a student of French bureaucracy has suggested that much of the enervating corruption that characterized the conduct of government during the Third Republic, as, for example, the Stavisky scandal, could have been avoided if the French Chamber of Deputies had possessed adequate powers of inquiry into matters of administration.[12] But of course Teapot Dome and other episodes in the history of American bureaucracy suggest that the possibility of exposure is not in itself sufficient to prevent administrative scandal in our own society.

In its criticism of executive secrecy, the legislature has always drawn strong support from a powerful constellation of interests in American society—the organized associations of newspaper editors and publishers. This support includes such organizations as the American Society of Newspaper Editors, the American Newspaper Publishers Association, and the Associated Press Managing Editors Association. For reasons of economic self-interest as well as ideological dedication to a free press, the newspaper industry's condemnation of governmental secrecy has been even more sweeping and persistent than that of the legislature. (It includes legislative secrecy among its targets.) The passage of resolutions attacking governmental secrecy has now become standard fare whenever newspapermen meet in state or national conventions.

The general view of the newspaper industry has been that the people have a "right to know," [13] and that this right can

[11] Harry Street, "State Secrets—A Comparative Study," *Modern Law Review*, Vol. 14 (April, 1951), pp. 121–35. The leading British case is *Duncan v. Cammell, Laird & Co.*, A.C. 624 (1942).

[12] Henry W. Ehrmann, "The Duty of Disclosure in Parliamentary Investigation: A Comparative Study," *Chicago Law Review*, Vol. 11 (December, 1943; February, 1944), pp. 1–25, 117–53.

[13] This title is attached to the most definitive statement of the journalist's view on this question, Harold L. Cross, *The People's Right to Know—Legal Access to Public Records and Proceedings* (New York, 1953).

only be enforced if the institutions upon which the people depend for news have access to government officials and government records. The press thus prides itself upon playing a role as agent of the people in the continuous struggle it has carried on against the development of secrecy in administration, a struggle that has extended to all phases of government activity, save where matters of defense or national security are involved, and even here the press has been skeptical of the uses to which the privilege of secrecy might be put.

Other media of communication, including radio, television, and the periodical press, have joined newspaper groups in a continuing fight upon executive secrecy. While all segments of the news industry thus stand together in demanding access to official information, there is of course some conflict of interest among them. The newspapers, for example, are somewhat less enthusiastic about advancing the newer efforts of radio and television reporters to gather information than they are in protecting their own competitive and more traditional privileges.

As a matter of fact, the television camera still has not gained the same right of attendance at official proceedings as that which has traditionally been accorded the journalist. Cameramen, both newsreel and television, are at something of a disadvantage in gaining access to such meetings, since their presence often demands the introduction of cumbersome and perhaps distracting equipment—which may require considerably more in the way of a concession on the part of a government official than the attendance of a newspaper reporter carrying a pad and pencil. These photographers are also more vulnerable to control, since they may be denied effective access to a government building by the simple expedient of an official refusal to co-operate in hooking up their equipment.

The strong interest the press takes in executive secrecy helps insure widespread newspaper coverage of legislative attacks upon the withholding of information. For several years now, the House Subcommittee on Government Information has been conducting a critical inquiry into administrative secrecy, and one of its minority members has taken public notice of the benefits accruing to its chairman, Representative Moss, of California, from the nationwide publicity given the committee's activities:

> Whatever the chairman's intent may have been, the effect of this subcommittee's conspiracy with the press has been his personal glorification. The effectiveness of this press agentry may be evident in Mr. Moss's success in capturing both the Democratic and Republican nominations in California's Third Congressional District.[14]

The desire of the press to open up channels of information extends to state as well as national government, and during recent years newspaper groups have been instrumental in bringing about the passage of laws limiting governmental secrecy in a number of states, including Illinois, Ohio, and Pennsylvania.[15]

Since World War II, executive secrecy has also come under increasingly heavy fire from the scientific community in this country. This criticism has its roots in the growing involvement of the federal government in scientific research—an involvement that has brought technical development in many fields, particularly atomic energy, under substantial government control. Today scientists in and out of the public service have a vested interest in governmental procedures and policies with respect to the release of information in their professional field. In this area the web of executive secrecy extends beyond government itself and embraces projects operated by private institutions under official auspices.

Much of the scientists' criticism of secrecy rests on the

---

[14] *Thirty-Fifth Report by the Committee on Government Operations,* 85th Cong. 2d Sess., House Report No. 2578, Aug. 13, 1958, p. 243.

[15] See *New York Times,* June 23, 1957; July 12, 1957.

premise that it is unnecessary, because it attempts to conceal matters that are part of the general fund of scientific knowledge in the Western world or that can be easily discovered by scientists working outside the classification system. There is, of course, general agreement that the weapons developed through modern science may themselves need to be kept secret, but as one scientist put it:

A field as basic as that of magnetism is known to all competent scientists throughout the world already. If there is something new ready to be discovered in that field, it will also be discovered by people in other countries. An attempt to keep such a discovery secret in this country would handicap ourselves, I am sure, more than it would withhold from others.[16]

One striking fact which this comment points up is the changing character of the so-called "state secret." In the past such secrets dealt mainly with purely military matters—troop dispositions, fortifications, battle plans, and the like. This was information that a potential adversary could obtain only through espionage. Now, increasingly, even the strictest counterintelligence measures cannot hide a secret that an enemy can uncover through scientific research and exploration in his own laboratory. Of course, if one scientific community keeps its inventions secret, it may be able to delay the speed with which another society is able to make comparable discoveries. This is one of the compelling considerations that has led to the proliferation of restrictions on the disclosure of scientific information. But insofar as such restrictions serve to stimulate more intensive counter efforts toward secrecy or toward fresh discoveries in rival camps, they may yield little or no net advantage. And the U-2 affair provides impressive evidence of the stimulus secrecy gives to retaliatory espionage.

[16] See *Twenty-Third Report by the Committee on Government Operations*, 85th Cong. 2d Sess., House Report No. 1619, April 22, 1958, p. 21.

The difficulty of keeping secrets is related to what is perhaps the most basic of all scientific criticisms of governmental secrecy. This is the charge that it has become unduly negative in character through its stress upon the necessity of concealing rather than uncovering information. In the view of an influential part of the scientific community, innovation and development depend essentially upon a widespread flow of communications among scientists working on related problems. Insofar as governmental secrecy stifles such communication, it hampers scientific progress. From this perspective, the benefits to be gained in terms of a high rate of scientific discovery more than offset whatever element of risk may be present in removing restrictions on communications. Scientific achievement is itself regarded as the firmest basis for national security.

Not the least of the advantages of a policy of maximum disclosure is the fact that it strengthens the possibility of chance discovery, which has played so important a role in the history of science, and assists in the "hot pursuit" of a scientific problem from its genesis to its solution. As one scientist has noted:

> . . . The really significant new concepts of science are often, if not always, the result of association of widely diverse facts and ideas that may not hitherto have seemed remotely connected.
>
> Such ideas as the laws of mechanics and the concepts of space and time derived from astronomy, together with the work of Planck on high temperature radiation, led Einstein to postulate the equivalence of mass and energy. On this concept is based the development of nuclear energy.
>
> Yet today, any intelligent military organization, operating under the present security rules, would certainly classify the equivalent of Planck's work so that it would be denied to a potential Einstein.[17]

[17] See *Hearings:* House Subcommittee on Government Information, 84th Cong. 2d Sess., Mar. 7, 8, 9, 1956, p. 756.

Needless to say, reasonable men still disagree as to whether or
not the gain in terms of a high rate of discovery equal or offset
the loss that may be involved in opening up a one-way system
of communications with a potential national adversary.

The direct and indirect support given the legislative attack
upon executive secrecy by both the press and the scientific
community reflects the wide variety of interests served by
efforts to prevent the withholding of executive information.
Students of political institutions themselves have perhaps the
greatest stake in the success of legislative efforts to expose the
processes of government to relentless scrutiny, since disclosure
in this instance may be an indispensable aid to effective schol-
arship. But it should here be noted that each of the groups that
has been active in support of the tradition of publicity can
also point to a clear public interest in the success of its special
efforts. For the public has an obvious stake in the effective
performance of the legislative task, as it does in the availability
of information in the hands of executive officials to the media
of communications upon which the people depend for knowledge concerning the affairs of government. And the public
has no less an interest in keeping open the channels of communications upon which the economic progress of society
may be said to depend.

In view of the cumulative strength of these considerations
it is not surprising that it could be said of American government as it has traditionally been operated that: "Within the
government, secrecy was at a minimum until the Second
World War. Even the military, which in liberal societies is
the chief locus of secrecy, was not granted many prerogatives
in this respect in the United States nor did it aspire to
them. . . . Within the civilian branches of the government,
where secrecy had even feebler roots, 'security-consciousness'
was very faint." [18] Over much of its history, American ad-

[18] Shils, *op. cit.*, p. 42.

ministration has thus provided something of an exception to Weber's stereotype of bureaucracy as a system of organization inevitably characterized by a high degree of secrecy.

The Onset of Secrecy

Recent years, which have been productive of so many changes in the scope and character of American government, have seen the emergence of a substantial number of pressures directed at increasing the extent of secrecy prevailing in the conduct of American administration. The most visible if not the most important of these factors has of course been the full-scale involvement of the United States in world politics and, more recently, in the cold war with the Soviet Union and its satellites. The expanded commitments of the United States in diplomatic and military affairs would alone have brought about a very considerable increase in pressure towards administrative secrecy, but to this development there has been added the fact that advances in modern science and technology have enormously widened the range of subjects that need to be kept safe from disclosure in the interest of maintaining a military or diplomatic advantage. State secrets are, therefore, both more important and more numerous in the operations of contemporary American government.

No less important, though less visible, are the other factors which have contributed to the growth of secrecy in American administration. There is in fact no major segment of the administrative process as it has continued to develop in recent years that has remained unaffected by this pressure. The expanded scope of governmental regulation in the economic sphere has, for example, brought about an increased need for secrecy in the area of regulatory administration. The resort to secrecy in the enforcement of regulatory statutes is the product of such factors as the desire to protect those subject 2, to regulation from adverse publicity when a suspected violation of the law is still under investigation, as well as the need 3, to insure the government itself from premature disclosure of its investigative efforts where it is moving toward prosecution. The reasons for secrecy in law enforcement were summarized very well in an opinion written by Attorney General Jackson in 1941. Jackson noted that disclosure of confidential data in law enforcement files might tip off criminals under investigation, could embarrass and might even endanger confidential informants, and, in view of the erroneous information and malicious gossip often contained in investigative reports, "might also be the grossest kind of injustice to innocent individuals." [19]

Moreover, in connection with a number of its activities, the government now comes into possession of countless records of private citizens and business firms containing material such as trade secrets and financial data, which it would be most disadvantageous for the parties concerned to have divulged. In fact much of this information is filed with the government with the expectation that it will not become a matter of public knowledge, and a substantial number of private groups have thus acquired a vested interest in governmental secrecy. For example, the Housing and Home Finance Agency follows the practice of withholding credit information submitted by mortgagors to the FHA, and the Department of Labor gives a similar confidential status to data furnished by employers or job applicants to one of its employment offices. Drug manufacturers are required to file a great deal of information of a trade secret character with the Food and Drug Administration, and this material is also withheld from public inspection as are the records of wage earners under the Social Security program.

There are in fact many pressures which conspire to move

[19] *Official Opinions of the Attorneys General*, Vol. 40, p. 45.

government in a secretive direction as it becomes increasingly active in the economic sphere. One observer has even argued that administrative secrecy will necessarily be a central characteristic of a government which attempts central direction and control of the economy.[20] It is clear at least that the timing of governmental decisions having an economic effect may be of critical importance in a managed economy, and this fact may force the introduction of strict regulations prohibiting any premature disclosure of pending decisions. During World War II, for example, OPA decisions on changes in the rationing system had to be kept closely guarded secrets before their scheduled announcement in order to discourage hoarding on the part of consumers. And monetary authorities have commonly had to resort to secrecy in connection with their deliberations on changes in currency and credit regulations.

Moreover, in this country government operations in the economic sphere are often modeled after practices which prevail in the private sector of the economy, in part because these activities may be administered by officials drawn from the ranks of private industry. As a result a good deal of ordinary business secrecy has come to be assimilated into the procedures of executive agencies. The Moss subcommittee on Government Information has entered a stringent criticism of this tendency in the operation of the Defense Department:

> The tendency to apply business secrecy to public matters is illustrated by . . . the handling of leases negotiated by private firms for commercial space in the Pentagon. Some 20 private firms, including a department store, drugstore, and bank, occupy space on the concourse in the Pentagon to do business with the 30,000 virtual "captive" consumers employed there. The selected firms pay a percentage of their receipts to the Govern-

[20] Lon L. Fuller, "Governmental Secrecy and the Forms of Social Order," in *Community, Nomos* II, edited by Carl J. Friedrich (New York, 1959), pp. 256–68.

ment as rent. Until the subcommittee made an issue of it because of complaints from the press, the Defense Department negotiated the leases in secret and kept the terms of the leases secret.[21]

While this policy of secrecy was eventually abandoned by the Pentagon, it was stoutly defended by the general counsel of the department on the grounds that it followed procedures practiced by private businesses all over the country.

Personnel administration, which has widened in its scope as government has increased in its size, has also contributed to the growth of administrative secrecy. The Civil Service Commission, along with other administrative units charged with responsibility for matters of personnel, is faced with the necessity of maintaining the secrecy of much of the expanding mass of material it has accumulated in connection with its recruitment of government employees. Testing materials as well as the names and records of applicants for government positions and investigative and medical reports on such applicants are among the matters that are kept from public disclosure as a matter of official policy. It is recognized that disclosure of certain kinds of material in personnel files might bring damage to an applicant for government employment, at the minimum perhaps supplying to his employer the information that he is in fact looking for another job, or at the worst publicizing facts about his personal life that may be highly embarrassing to him. Consequently, from the point of view of a personnel agency itself, the maintenance of guarantees of secrecy on job applications is regarded as indispensable for the successful operation of a recruitment program.

The mere growth in the size and complexity of the executive branch of the government in recent years has itself brought about increased pressure toward administrative secrecy. An expanding bureaucracy, proliferating in a variety

[21] *Twenty-Seventh Report by the Committee on Government Operations,* 85th Cong. 2d Sess. House Report No. 1884, June 16, 1958, p. 6.

of directions, develops a voluminous flow of communications between and within administrative agencies. These communications include such matters as interdepartmental memoranda, advisory opinions, policy recommendations, tentative plans and proposals, the minutes of committee meetings, and oral advice. Much of this material has come to be considered by the executive branch as immune from outside inspection for, among other reasons, the purpose of encouraging candor on the part of administrative officials in speaking their minds. The confidential status thus accorded internal communications assures administrative officials that unpopular views which they express will not subject them to congressional or public attack. As subsequent discussion will show, American presidents have traditionally felt that the privacy surrounding administrative deliberations is indispensable for the efficient conduct of executive affairs.

It is of course also true that an expanding bureaucracy tends to develop a more highly refined division of labor, and at least one aspect of this development has contributed to the growth of administrative secrecy. The specialization of the public information function leads to a centralization of control in one office over the flow of communications from administration to the public. While from an executive point of view the institutionalization of reporting or public relations activity is designed to achieve such vital objectives as the co-ordination of policy statements coming from an administrative agency, it inevitably tends also to reduce access to information by closing off sources of news other than the public information unit itself. The net effect of this practice is to cloak from public scrutiny an important segment of the policy-making process, insofar as the internal deliberations of administrative agencies have come to play an increasingly important role in shaping as well as executing government decisions.

Many agencies have laid down regulations making it a mis-demeanor for subordinate officials to release information to the press, apart from those specifically authorized to do so. The Civil Service Commission, for example, has a rule prohibiting its employees from divulging information concerning internal disputes within the agency or between the commission and other governmental units. In 1955 the Department of Defense handed down a directive (since repealed) which specified that information should be released only when it constituted "a constructive contribution to the primary mission of the Department of Defense." And the State Department, on April 4, 1958, issued a circular restricting the contacts of its research and intelligence personnel with the press to those occasions when a public information officer could be present. The department also instituted the practice of requiring its employees to file a memo on meetings with reporters, a requirement that may do much to prevent the unauthorized release of information.

There is another factor which has to be considered in evaluating the effect of public relations activity upon the availability of information from government agencies. This is the fact that a public information unit has as one of its principal functions the advancement of the public stature and prestige of the administrative agency within which it is located. Such an office has, therefore, a vested interest in confining the release of information to material which will reflect credit upon the agency. Thus, while the immediate effect of the establishment of a public information unit may be to increase the quantity of communications flowing from an executive agency to the public, the character of this information can be expected to become much more favorable to the agency concerned. It is for this reason that Congress and the news media have tended to look upon the creation of public information offices as obstructing rather than facilitating public knowledge of executive operations. The principal function of a public information unit has, in fact, come to be regarded in these quarters as that of preventing the disclosure of information which may prove politically embarrassing to an executive agency. Some observers have even suggested that the best way to widen the flow of useful information to the public is to abolish all government information offices. Witness the following comment:

> Indeed, it might be that if some of the information offices could be legislated out of existence, the press and the public—and perhaps Congress itself—would get more and better information through direct contact with the policymakers and workers of the executive departments, unimpeded by press agents whose instinct is to see every situation through their own rose-colored glasses.[22]

Secrecy and Efficiency

One fact which the trend toward withholding information makes abundantly clear is the widespread conviction that secrecy serves the public interest by contributing to administrative efficiency. This argument crops up repeatedly, not only with respect to defense and foreign policy, where secrecy presents an obvious barrier to espionage, but also in areas of domestic policy where matters of national security are not even remotely involved. For a long time the Post Office Department followed the practice of refusing to make public the names of individuals who had passed a preliminary examination and become eligible for appointment as local postmasters. The department defended this policy on the grounds that it prevented the possibility of later embarrassment to those who were not subsequently offered appointments and in this way increased the number of those willing to apply for the position of postmaster. As the assistant postmaster general put it:

[22] See *Hearings:* House Subcommittee on Government Information, 84th Cong., 1st sess., Nov. 7, 1955, p. 31.

In my opinion, we are getting a little better caliber and more applicants as a result of the withholding of the registers. I realize what is in the public interest is a matter of judgment. Is it more in the public interest to get the best candidates for postmasters, or to satisfy entirely the public curiosity about the candidates for postmasters? It is a difficult question to answer, and my own experience in the field of personnel administration makes me absolutely certain that the publication of the names of applicants for almost any position that is not elective causes great difficulty in getting higher caliber personnel to make those applications.[23]

Eventually, however, under congressional pressure the department retreated from this policy and asked the Civil Service Commission to disclose the names of qualified applicants to the public.

In this case, as in others, it may well be a moot point as to whether secrecy is as vital to the success of an administrative enterprise as an executive official may think it is. The fact that a policy is convenient or saves embarrassment is not necessarily an indication that it contributes to administrative efficiency. In the case cited above, the assistant postmaster general was not able to show that the department's recruitment efforts had been notably more successful under a policy of secrecy than had otherwise been the case. But it still remains true that in areas of governmental activity where government agencies depend upon the voluntary response of private citizens, occasions may arise when the co-operation of these citizens can be obtained only by serving their convenience or sparing them from personal embarrassment.

Of course the impact of secrecy upon the effectiveness of governmental agencies needs always to be weighed against its simultaneous effects upon their responsiveness to public observation and control. For in democratic societies the ap-

[23] See *Hearings:* House Subcommittee on Government Information, 84th Cong. 1st Sess., November 8, 9, 10, 1955, pp. 169–70.

propriateness of administrative rules and procedures cannot be measured entirely by the degree to which they contribute to the competence with which the tasks of government are performed. Responsiveness no less than competence is the hallmark of a successfully functioning democratic bureaucracy. And a practice of secrecy may so weaken the responsiveness of governmental machinery to popular control that no gain it may appear to afford in administrative effectiveness is worth the price, taking also into account the fact that the gain may in any case be an illusory one.

Whatever else is true, the factors that have contributed to the growth of administrative secrecy represent trends that do not, at least in the visible future, appear likely to be reversed. This would certainly seem to be true with respect to such developments as the cold war, the expansion of bureaucracy, the widening range of regulatory activity, and the preoccupation of administrative agencies with good public relations. Since these trends will undoubtedly continue, it can rather be expected that pressure toward secrecy in administration will increase rather than diminish with time. This fact has given special urgency to the problem of reconciling the legitimate public and private interests served by the practice of withholding information with the very real stake of the community in preserving the tradition of disclosure with respect to governmental affairs.

Since administrative secrecy depends to some degree upon decisions and actions taken in the legislature, the executive, and the judiciary alike, it is a problem that has loomed large on the agenda of each of these major institutions of American government. In the chapters that follow, an attempt will be made to trace the part played by Congress, the president, and the courts in promoting or limiting the practice of secrecy by administrative agencies. But it should here be noted that there is no more impressive evidence of the strength of the trend toward administrative secrecy in contemporary American government than the fact that legislative and judicial as well as presidential blessing have so often been given to its continued development.

CHAPTER 3

THE CONGRESSIONAL DILEMMA

ON THE SURFACE at least, it might appear that
Congress would be altogether opposed to the growth of administrative secrecy, since attacks upon this practice are so
common a feature of congressional politics. By resolution, investigation, and the threat of even more punitive sanctions,
the national legislature has repeatedly asserted its belief that
executive officials should not be allowed to withhold documents and testimony at their own discretion.[1] The most visible
evidence of recent legislative concern in this regard has been
provided by the activities of Congressman Moss's Special Subcommittee on Government Information, which has made far-
ranging efforts to expose and dramatize the evils of executive
secrecy.[2] Over the past five years, the Subcommittee on Con-

[1] For a description of some of the principal episodes in this conflict see
Wilfred Binkley, *The President and Congress* (New York, 1947). A recent
tabulation of controversies in this area from the time of Washington to the
present day may be found in *The Power of the President to Withhold Information from the Congress*, Memorandums of the Attorney-General, Compiled by the Sub-Committee on Constitutional Rights of the Senate Committee on the Judiciary, 85th Cong., 2d Sess., Feb. 6, 1958; Oct. 31, 1958.

[2] The House Subcommittee has held hearings periodically since November 7, 1955, and has issued interim reports since that time. The work of the
Committee up to July, 1960, is summarized in three progress reports, *Twenty-
Fifth Intermediate Report of the Committee on Government Operations*,
84th Cong., 2d sess., House Report No. 2947, July 27, 1956; *Thirty-Fifth Re-*

stitutional Rights of the Senate Committee on the Judiciary has also carried on extensive investigations in this area.[3]

The long standing congressional resentment against administrative efforts to conceal information has been expressed in connection with a wide range of executive activities. In the field of defense policy, especially, congressional dependence upon executive information is acute, and bitter controversy has been sparked by executive refusals to release data bearing on such matters as the missile program, foreign aid expenditures, and differences within the high command over the best way to spend the defense dollar.[4]

Among recent instances where Congress has found executive secrecy a handicap in its efforts to oversee administration, none has gained more publicity than the Dixon-Yates affair. In 1955 congressional critics of the administration's proposals to finance private construction of a utility plant to feed power into the Tennessee Valley Authority system for the benefit of the AEC were exercised to discover that a Bureau of the Budget consultant, Adolphe H. Wenzell, had simultaneously been an officer of the First Boston Corporation. This was the financial institution that had represented Dixon-Yates in negotiations with the AEC and the Budget Bureau.

Although the administration at first insisted that Wenzell had not actually participated in contract discussions, subsequent inquiry disclosed that he had indeed played the role of

port by the Committee on Government Operations, 85th Cong., 2d sess., House Report No. 2578, August 13, 1958; and Twenty-Fourth Report by the Committee on Government Operations, 86th Cong., 2d sess., House Report No. 2084, July 2, 1960.

[3] See, for example, the studies and hearings listed in Publication Relating to the Work of the Sub-Committee on Constitutional Rights, 86th Cong., 1st sess., Committee Print, November 1, 1959.

[4] Many of the principal issues that have arisen in the area of defense policy are discussed in an interim report by the Moss subcommittee. Twenty-Seventh Report by the Committee on Government Operations, 85th Cong., 2d sess., House Report No. 1884, June 16, 1958.

intermediary in the affair.[5] The difficulty Congress encountered in obtaining accurate information on this and other matters connected with the Dixon-Yates investigation prompted Senator O'Mahoney to the conclusion that "there has been an utmost effort on the part of witnesses from the government to conceal the facts." Among the government officials who refused at one point or another to give testimony on their part in contract negotiations were the Budget Director, Rowland Hughes; the chairman of the Atomic Energy Commission, Lewis L. Strauss; the chairman of the Securities and Exchange Commission, J. Sinclair Armstrong; and Presidential Assistant Sherman Adams.[6]

Testimony to the continued strength of the congressional determination to preserve access to data in the hands of executive officials may also be found in the refusal of the Senate in 1959 to confirm the nomination of Lewis L. Strauss to be secretary of commerce—an event which marked only the eighth time in our history that a cabinet nominee had been denied confirmation. One of the principal charges levelled against Strauss was the accusation that he had made excessive use of the doctrine of executive privilege to withhold information from the legislature—a refusal Congress believed was based principally on the damage that disclosure might do to Strauss's own reputation. Senator Anderson, a leader of the opposition, called the rejection of Mr. Strauss "a signal victory

[5] The AEC itself was subsequently to admit this when it held the contract invalid on the grounds of Wenzell's conflicting private interest. As the agency put it: "The matters on which Wenzell was advising the contractor (Dixon) were the same on which he had been employed to advise the government." In a decision reimbursing Dixon-Yates for out-of-pocket costs before the contract was cancelled, the Court of Claims later ruled that the activities of Wenzell did not represent a genuine conflict of interest. *Mississippi Valley Generating Co.* v. *United States,* 175 F. Supp. 505 (1959). However, upon appeal the AEC was eventually upheld by the Supreme Court. *United States* v. *Mississippi Valley Generating Co.,* 81 S. Ct. 294 (1961).

[6] For a summary of the Dixon-Yates dispute, see the *Congressional Quarterly Almanac,* Vol. 11 (1955), pp. 533–38.

for those who still believe this is a government for the people and that the public should be protected against a man who might use executive privilege to hide the truth." [7]

One issue that has generated persistent heat over a period spanning the terms of the last three presidents has been the question of congressional inspection of loyalty-security files. Roosevelt, Truman, and Eisenhower have each in turn had occasion to exercise their presidential prerogative to refuse Congress permission to inspect documents bearing on such matters.[8] This refusal has been based partly on a desire to protect the individuals whose records were requested from the damage they might incur through the exposure of some of the material contained in their files—scurrilous accusations, for example. It has also been justified on the grounds that secrecy is necessary for the efficient administration of the loyalty-security program, since it protects the identity of confidential informants to the government from a disclosure that might jeopardize their usefulness.

Pressure to obtain material contained in these files has come mainly from the conservative sectors of the legislature—in both the Democratic and the Republican parties. But the notion of open government is at least as much a liberal as it is a conservative doctrine. The assaults upon secrecy in both the Dixon-Yates and Strauss affairs were mounted mainly by legislators of liberal persuasion, and two of the chief protagonists of the "people's right to know," Congressman Moss, of California, and (until his death in 1960) Senator Hennings, of Missouri, would generally be classified as liberal in political outlook. Moreover, the fight against secrecy has been pushed with equal vigor whether Congress was under Democratic or

[7] See *New York Times*, June 20, 1959, p. 8.
[8] See the memorandum from Attorney-General Brownell to President Eisenhower as printed in *Replies from Federal Agencies to Questionnaire Submitted by the Special Sub-committee on Government Information*, 84th Cong., 1st sess., November 1, 1955, pp. 546–52.

Republican control. Antagonism to executive secrecy is thus an issue upon which all ideological and partisan factions in the legislature can make common cause.

Support for Secrecy

The paradoxical fact is, however, that while the cause of open government owes much to the legislative effort to uproot executive secrecy, Congress itself is responsible in no small measure for the extent to which the practice of withholding information has become a characteristic feature of executive operations. Time and again the groups allied with Congress in the struggle for a less restrictive policy on the release of information have found a cluster of statutes imbedded at the root of executive secrecy, even where such secrecy is also grounded on the claim of executive privilege or presidential directive. In its investigations of government secrecy the Moss subcommittee found that government agencies could refer to a wide range of statutes in defense of the practice of withholding information. The Department of Agriculture, for example, was able to cite no less than fifteen laws, including the Commodity Exchange Act, Tobacco Stocks and Standards Act, and Agricultural Adjustment Act of 1938, as amended.[9]

Congressional protection for administrative secrecy has come in part from legislation of general application to all executive agencies. Of central and pervasive significance in this regard is the so-called housekeeping power that has been vested in the heads of executive departments. As stated in the basic law underlying the organization of these agencies:

> The head of each department is authorized to prescribe regulations, not inconsistent with law, for the government of his department, the conduct of its officers and clerks, the distribution

[9] *Ibid.,* pp. 7–10.

and performance of its business, and the custody, use and preservation of its records, papers, and property appertaining to it.[10]

The significant clause here is of course that pertaining to "the custody, use and preservation" of administrative records. Under this general statutory authority, the heads of executive agencies have promulgated a variety of regulations designed to prevent subordinate administrative officials from public disclosure of information to which they have official access. These regulations have been applied both to maintain the secrecy of information obtained from private individuals having dealings with the government and to safeguard the confidential character of internal communications within administration.

Although the legality of regulations of this character has been questioned as being inconsistent with the statutory authority on which they are based, such challenges have been uniformly unsuccessful in court. The view of the judiciary has been that an administrative regulation prohibiting the disclosure of official information is plainly within the statutory authority vested in the head of an executive agency by Congress. Typical of such regulations is one that has been issued by the attorney-general to safeguard the confidential character of material contained within the files of the Department of Justice:

> All official files, documents, records and information in the offices of the Department of Justice, including the several offices of United States Attorneys, Federal Bureau of Investigation, United States Marshals, and Federal penal and correctional institutions, or in the custody and control of any officer or employee of the Department of Justice, are to be regarded as confidential. No officer or employee may permit the disclosure or use of the same for any purpose other than for the performance of his

[10] 5 U.S.C.A. § 22. For amendment of this statute, however, see below pp. 58–60.

official duties, except in the discretion of the Attorney-General, the Assistant to the Attorney General, or an Assistant Attorney General acting for him.

Whenever a subpoena *duces tecum* is served to produce any of such files, documents, records or information, the officer or employee on whom such subpoena is served, unless otherwise expressly directed by the Attorney-General, will appear in court to answer thereto and respectfully decline to produce the records specified therein, on the ground that disclosure of such records is prohibited by this regulation.[11]

Acting upon this regulation, officials of the Department of Justice have in fact refused to produce information requested in judicial proceedings, and their right to do so has been upheld by the Supreme Court.

It has also been long-standing congressional practice to provide special statutory protection for the privacy of certain kinds of business information in the hands of government officials when its release might inflict undeserved economic injury or provide windfall benefits. Laws establishing regulatory agencies, such as the FTC and the SEC, commonly contain provisions designed to prevent government employees from disclosing information regarding the internal affairs of business firms under their jurisdiction. A statute enacted in 1948 applies this prohibition generally to all government agencies:

Whoever, being an officer or employee of the United States or of any department or agency thereof, publishes, divulges, discloses, or makes known in any manner or to any extent not authorized by law any information coming to him in the course of his employment or official duties . . . shall be fined not more than $1,000 or imprisoned not more than one year, or both; and shall be removed from office or employment.[12]

[11] Federal Register, Vol. 11, No. 8 (May 4, 1946), p. 4920.
[12] 18 U.S.C. § 1905.

Laws of this kind ordinarily provide a business firm with some protection against having trade secrets, technical processes, or financial records disclosed to business rivals, and they help government agencies obtain the trade co-operation needed for the collection of statistical data.

Such statutes also attempt to insure against the possibility that a government official may use information that comes to him in his official capacity for personal economic advantage, or may assist others in doing so. The nature of this problem was pointed up in 1956 by a congressional investigation into the fact that several investors had made quick profits on Northeast Airlines stock after they received advance information that the Civil Aeronautics Board was about to award a highly prized and supposedly lucrative New York-to-Miami route to Northeast. The chairman of the CAB, in asking Congress for legislation to curb these leaks, declared that such disclosures had plagued his agency for years.[13] The problem of preventing the advance release of information having value in market speculation is a particular problem for regulatory agencies such as the CAB and the SEC, but it also arises in other areas of administration, as for example, in connection with the release of crop reports by the USDA.[14] Nor is it confined to executive agencies; judicial decisions on tax matters present similar problems.

Since World War II, congressional support for executive secrecy has put great emphasis upon preventing the disclosure of information affecting the national security. The Atomic Energy Act of 1946, for example, represented a novel attempt to define one entire area of information that was to be subject

[13] The Congressional investigation of this CAB leak was carried on under the direction of Senator Henry Jackson. See *Leaks of CAB Decision of August 2, 1956 Affecting Northeast Airlines Stock,* 85th Cong., 1st sess., May 1–21, 1957.

[14] The secrecy of crop reports is protected by 18 U.S.C. § 1902.

to stringent government control.[15] In enacting this law, Congress included detailed provisions designed to prevent and punish the unauthorized release of information by employees of the Atomic Energy Commission. The scope of the information thus prohibited from disclosure is very broad: it includes "all data concerning the manufacture or utilization of atomic weapons, the production of fissionable material, or the use of fissionable material in the production of power." Administrative officials found guilty of violating this statute face formidable penalties, including, in certain cases, a death sentence.

Pursuant to a recommendation of the United States Commission on Government Security (four of whose twelve members were congressmen), legislation was also introduced in 1957 which would have extended the criminal penalties attached to espionage to cover reporters and others outside the government who released official information that had not been authorized for publication.[16] This legislation provoked widespread criticism from newspapers across the country, particularly after the chairman of the commission had publicly chastised the press for the "dark chapters of betrayal" it had written in American history, and the bill has not subsequently been acted upon by Congress.[17] Writing in the *New York Times*, James Reston noted that under the terms of this bill, newsmen would have been liable to prosecution for the exposure of skulduggery in both the Teapot Dome and Dixon-Yates affairs.

[15] See in this connection, James R. Newman, "Control of Information relating to Atomic Energy," *Yale Law Journal*, Vol. 56 (May, 1947), pp. 769–802. The 1954 amendments to the act went some distance toward relaxing this control. See Herbert S. Marks and George F. Trowbridge, "Control of Information under the Atomic Energy Act of 1954," *Bulletin of the Atomic Scientists*, Vol. 11 (April, 1955), pp. 128–30.

[16] See United States Commission on Government Security, *Report*, Washington, GPO, 1957.

[17] *New York Times*, July 1, 1957.

The Jencks Case

Recent years have seen no more dramatic proof of the
willingness of Congress to align itself on the side of secrecy in
at least some areas of executive operations than the series of
events which ensued in the wake of the decision of the Supreme Court in the case of *Jencks* v. *United States*.[18] For two
and one-half months following this decision, hardly a day
went by without an expression of legislative apprehension
over the jeopardy in which the Court's decision was believed
to have placed vital administrative secrets. This anxiety was
finally to culminate in the passage of a bill designed to restrict
if not eliminate the possibility that confidential executive records might be exposed to public scrutiny.

The Supreme Court decision which triggered this response
was handed down on June 3, 1957. It had its origins in the
conviction of a union organizer, Clifford Jencks, for false statements on a noncommunist affidavit submitted under the terms
of the Taft-Hartley Act. During his trial, two government
witnesses testified that Jencks had engaged in communist activities during the period covered by the affidavit. The defense
thereupon sought access to reports these witnesses had made
to the FBI contemporaneously with the events concerning
which they had testified at the trial. The refusal of the trial
judge to grant this request was upheld by the circuit court
upon appeal.[19] In the view of these lower courts, a request of
this kind could only be granted when the defense made some
showing of inconsistency between these earlier reports and
testimony given at a trial. This conclusion was in good part
based upon earlier Supreme Court decisions in which access
to government records had been denied.[20]

[18] 353 U.S. 657 (1957).
[19] 226 F. 2d. 540 (1955).
[20] Particularly *Gordon* v. *United States,* 344 U.S. 414 (1953).

But the Supreme Court, in handing down the Jencks decision, ruled that its earlier opinions had been misconstrued and that no such inconsistency need necessarily be shown. While the need for disclosure was heightened by a showing of inconsistency between earlier reports of a witness and his trial testimony, it was not dependent upon it. Justice Brennan, who delivered the majority opinion, was of the further view that the defense should be given direct access to records bearing on a witness' testimony. Only in this way could a defense attorney determine whether or not these documents would be of material assistance in impeaching the testimony of government witnesses. However, Justice Burton, speaking for three justices who joined in a concurring opinion, argued that material from government files should first be presented for review by the presiding judge. The trial judge would thereafter be left with discretion to withhold documentary material if it did not appear relevant to the testimony in dispute, or if its exposure would jeopardize state secrets.

In a strongly worded dissent, Justice Clark said of the majority's opinion that it afforded the criminal "a Roman holiday for rummaging through confidential information as well as vital national secrets," and he predicted that the decision would open up "a veritable Pandora's box of troubles." This dissent had two rather remarkable features. In the first place it was not a very precise reading of the majority opinion. Justice Brennan had given explicit indication that the Court's opinion did not authorize any broad fishing expeditions into government files. The defense was to have access only to documents related to testimony given by a government witness.

And yet a second remarkable feature of this dissent was its prophetic character. For however narrow a construction the majority may have intended to put upon the right of inspection allowable under its decision, many lower courts proceeded to interpret the case as though Justice Clark's dissent was the authoritative reading of the Court's opinion. Some of these courts immediately adopted the view that the government must now turn over the entire body of its investigative reports to the defense, even though only a small part of this material may have actually been related to testimony given by a witness for the prosecution. Soon after the Jencks decision was handed down, a federal court in Atlanta ordered the government to come forward with its entire investigative report in a prevailing wage violation case. (Here the advantages of access would go not to a Communist but to a capitalist employer.) And in Pittsburgh an indictment was dismissed when the Narcotics Bureau refused to unveil its complete investigative files following the testimony of a government witness. Elsewhere similar decisions requiring wholesale disclosure were handed down.[21]

Moreover, some district judges jumped to the conclusion that the new ruling required the pre-trial discovery of information in government files. Actually the Court's opinion had touched only on a situation in which the defense sought access to documents after a government witness had testified at a trial and when it appeared that these documents might be useful in impeaching his testimony. This lower court expansion of the Jencks ruling to require pre-trial disclosure led one enterprising attorney in Texas to write the Department of Justice requesting that the entire government file on a pending case be mailed to him for his inspection. And when an FBI agent in Kentucky did not immediately accede to a court order directing him to furnish the defense with all documents, state-

[21] For summaries of lower court interpretations of the Jencks decision, see *Establishing Procedures for the Production of Government Records in Criminal Cases in United States Courts*, Senate Report No. 569, July 1, 1957, pp. 5–8; and *Establishing Procedures for the Production of Certain Government Records in Federal Criminal Cases*, 85th Cong., 1st sess., House Report No. 700, July 5, 1957, pp. 9–11. See also the *Congressional Record* for August 26, 1957, Vol. 103, No. 155, pp. 14551–54.

ments, and exhibits intended for use in a forthcoming trial, the court held that he was in civil contempt and fined him $1,000.

A swelling chorus of complaint against the Jencks decision and the implications being read into it by lower courts came welling up from Congress and in newspaper editorials across the country.[22] The dark forebodings contained in Clark's dissenting opinion seemed amply justified by events. The conviction spread that criminals, subversives, and other undesirables would soon be rooting about in government files—searching out the identity of confidential informants and obtaining leads on the investigative techniques followed by law enforcement agencies. Congress was particularly disturbed over the implications the decision might have for the activities of the FBI in the field of internal security. Ultimately, almost the entire legislative debate over the Jencks decision came to turn upon its effect on future prosecutions in the area of subversion and espionage. In point of fact, however, the immediate and apparent effects of the decision were most keenly felt in other less spectacular areas of federal criminal law enforcement.

To meet what the attorney-general of the United States called "a grave emergency in Federal law enforcement," no less than fourteen bills were introduced in Congress clarifying or limiting the effects of the Jencks decision. As its terms were eventually spelled out, the legislation adopted went a long way toward curbing expansive interpretations of the decision by lower courts. Under law the government is now required to disclose only those prior statements of a witness which relate to his testimony, and the defense can gain access to such re-

[22] For some representative congressional views, see the debates in the House on August 27, 1957, *Congressional Record*, Vol. 103, No. 156, pp. 14715–32. A sampling of unfavorable newspaper editorials may be found in the *Congressional Record* of August 26, 1957, pp. A7039, 7044, 7049, 7053, 7056. In interpreting the Jencks opinion, most of these editorials take their cue from the Clark dissent.

ports only after a witness has testified. In enacting this new law, Congress also threw its weight behind Justice Burton's concurring opinion and its restrained view on the procedure to be followed in granting disclosure. The records sought by the defense must first be screened by the presiding judge, who is given discretion to withhold material that appears unrelated to the testimony of the witness at a trial.

The furor aroused by the Jencks decision provides compelling evidence of the zeal with which Congress may spring to the defense of executive secrecy when official secrets and similar confidential matters are threatened with disclosure. Particularly worthy of note here is the fact that when the question of remedial legislation was being discussed, the attorney-general and other law enforcement officials in the executive branch actually asked for much less in the way of protection of their files than many congressmen were prepared to give. In this instance it was the legislature rather than the executive or the judiciary which led the way in protecting the secrecy of executive records. Moreover, the speed with which the bill was pushed through Congress led one senator to assert that "this ill-considered legislation is being rushed through the Senate without an adequate opportunity for all Senators to understand its real purport." [23]

Disclosure Legislation

In retrospect it is clear that however vigorous legislative attacks upon executive secrecy may occasionally be, Congress

---

[23] *Congressional Record*, Vol. 103, No. 148, August 15, 1957, pp. 13642. But the Supreme Court subsequently ruled that this legislation and not the Jencks decision now "governs the production of statements of government witnesses for a defendant's inspection at trial." *Rosenberg* v. *United States*, 79 S. Ct. 1231 (1959). See also *Palermo* v. *United States*, 79 S. Ct. 1217 (1959), and *Pittsburgh Plate Glass Company* v. *United States*, 79 S. Ct. 1237 (1959).

itself must bear much of the responsibility for the administrative practice of withholding information. A variety of statutes have been enacted which underwrite secrecy throughout the executive branch, while other laws protect segments of information lodged within the jurisdiction of particular agencies. In 1960 the House Subcommittee on Government Information listed 172 statutes which permit government information to be withheld from the public, as compared with 75 statutes which specifically require the dissemination of official data.

To be sure, the legislature has also enacted statutes pointed squarely in the direction of disclosure rather than secrecy. A principal objective of the Administrative Procedure Act of 1946 was to force executive agencies to disclose data bearing on such matters as their internal organization and distribution of authority. The legislative history of the act makes this point clearly with respect to the provisions relating to publicity:

> The section has been drawn upon the theory that administrative operations and procedures are public property which the general public, rather than a few specialists or lobbyists, is entitled to know or to have the ready means of knowing with definiteness and assurance.[24]

However, the Administrative Procedure Act, while generally requiring the publication by executive agencies of information relating to their organization, powers, and procedures, also identifies certain specific circumstances in which an agency may withhold information from public disclosure. According to the act, administrative secrecy is permissible where "there is involved (1) any function of the United States requiring secrecy in the public interest or (2) any matter relating solely to the internal management of an agency." To the extent that the protection thus afforded secrecy is

[24] *Administrative Procedure Act,* 79th Cong., 2d sess., Senate Document No. 248, July 26, 1946, p. 198.

found insufficient, administrative agencies may resort to the
further provision of the statute which states that information
should "be made available to persons properly and directly
concerned except information held confidential for good cause
found."

To some degree, of course, subsequent experience with the
publicity provisions of the Administrative Procedure Act reflects the success with which executive agencies contrive to
interpret statutes to suit their own convenience. Since the
law identifies several circumstances in which the publicity
requirement does not apply, executive agencies were quick to
rely on it as a general sanction for withholding rather than
disclosing information.[25] The Federal Reserve Board, for example, is one agency that has interpreted the publicity provisions of the law as permitting "nonpublication and nondisclosure of any information to the extent that it involves functions requiring nondisclosure in the public interest. . . .[26]

But the fate of the Administrative Procedure Act also testi-
fies to the fact that Congress is unwilling to write a general
statute requiring disclosure without at the same time making
ample provision for those occasions when the public interest
will demand that executive officials keep certain communications confidential. This point was made decisively clear in
1958, when congressional advocates of open government attempted to remove one of the chief statutory shields behind
which executive secrecy had traditionally been carried on—
the housekeeping act of 1789 which, as already noted, author-

[25] See in this regard *Replies from Federal Agencies to Questionnaire Submitted by the Special Sub-Committee on Government Information*, 84th
Cong., 1st sess., November 1, 1955. Legislation has been introduced in Congress
to amend the Administrative Procedure Act so as to prevent its being used
to justify secrecy. See the committee print issued by the subcommittee on
constitutional rights of the Senate Committee on the Judiciary, *A Bill to
Amend the Public Information Section of the Administrative Procedure Act*,
85th Cong., 2d sess.
[26] *Ibid.*, p. 197.

izes the heads of executive departments to control the "custody, use and preservation" of their own records.

This housekeeping act has been at the center of the struggle over executive secrecy for many years. It has figured in countless legal tests in which the courts have upheld the right of the head of an executive agency to forbid his subordinates to disclose information coming to them in their official capacity. The following statement from the legal representative of the American Society of Newspaper Editors is indicative of the importance attached to this statute by opponents of executive secrecy:

> This "housekeeping" statute, destitute as it is of all vestige of definitions and standards, is susceptible of being tortured, and has been tortured, with judicial sanction, it must be admitted, into a claim of privilege against disclosure and inspection so all encompassing that it may fairly be said that there is no hope of obtaining inspection of a public record not specifically opened by Congress except through the courtesy of the Government.[27]

From the beginning of its investigations in 1955, the House Subcommittee on Government Information singled out this statute as having been in large part responsible for the spread of executive secrecy.[28] In 1958, after more than two years of hearings and investigation, the subcommittee chairman, Representative Moss, introduced in Congress a bill to spell out the fact that the housekeeping law "does not authorize withholding information from the public or limiting the availability of records to the public." A companion bill was introduced by

[27] Harold L. Cross. *Hearings,* House Subcommittee on Government Information, 84th Cong., 1st sess., November 7, 1955, p. 12. Cross is a lifelong foe of government secrecy and, as previously indicated, the author of the most comprehensive legal study of the subject, *The People's Right to Know* (New York, 1953).

[28] See an article by the chief counsel of the Government Information Subcommittee, John J. Mitchell, "Government Secrecy in Theory and Practice: 'Rules and Regulations' As an Autonomous Screen," *Columbia Law Review,* Vol. 58 (February 1958), pp. 199–210.

Senator Hennings in the Senate. Support for this legislation came principally from newspaper groups, and it was opposed by each of the ten executive departments.[29] Ultimately, however, the bill was approved by both houses of Congress and signed by President Eisenhower.

However, before the bill finally became law, Representative Moss was obliged to assure his congressional colleagues that passage of his amendment would not endanger the secrecy of military and diplomatic records, income tax returns, trade secrets received by the government in confidence, Federal Bureau of Investigation reports, or information that could be withheld legitimately under other laws enacted by Congress.[30] In final effect the statute did little more than underline a point that judicial decision had sometimes left obscure —the fact that the housekeeping statute does not give the head of an executive department the right to withhold information, it merely grants him the authority to center decisions on the release of information in his own hands, thus withdrawing, if he chooses, discretion on such matters from the hands of subordinates. In a report issued in 1960, the Subcommittee on Government Information was later to admit that its amendment had not acted as an effective check upon executive secrecy.[31]

Congressional recognition of the need to allow some measure of executive secrecy was also visible in 1959, when an effort was made to amend the Mutual Security Appropriations Act of 1960 so as to cut off funds from the International Cooperation Administration when it refused legislative requests for information. This so-called "Hardy" amendment was inspired by congressional anger over the unwillingness of the

[29] See *Hearings*, House Subcommittee on Government Information, 85th Cong., 1st sess., February 6, 7, July 22, 1958.
[30] *New York Times*, April 17, 1958, p. 17.
[31] See *Twenty-Fourth Report by the Committee on Government Operations*, 86th Cong., 2d sess., House Report No. 2084. July 2, 1960, pp. 36-37.

ICA to furnish information on foreign aid programs in several countries, particularly Laos and Vietnam. However, as it was eventually passed by both houses of Congress, the amendment specifically stipulated that the ICA could still reject requests for information upon "a certification by the President that he has forbidden its being furnished."

Legislative Ambivalence

A fundamental ambivalence characterizes the legislative attempt to strike a balance between secrecy and publicity in administrative operations. Executive agencies may, for example, find themselves under simultaneous attack on the grounds that they are engaging in excessive secrecy and excessive publicity, hiding behind a "paper curtain of secrecy," while at the same time flooding the American public with a torrent of propaganda. In 1957 the Defense Department was caught in this legislative crossfire in connection with the abortive efforts to launch this country's first earth satellite. While the chairman of the House Subcommittee on Government Information was assailing the department for concealing the launching activity at Cape Canaveral, other legislators and newspapers across the country were taking the Defense Department to task for permitting any publicity in connection with this country's initial experiment with putting a satellite into orbit.

In the light of the record rather than the heat of congressional oratory, it can be seen that the legislature has done a good deal more to support the practice of executive secrecy than it has always been willing to admit. To be sure, congressional concessions to the need for secrecy in the executive process have come principally in the areas where state secrets are involved, or where a strong case can be made for withholding information to protect a property interest on the part of either government or a private citizen. Critics of the Atomic

Energy Act have contended that the legislature has, if anything, been too anxious to protect state secrets.[32]

The value that tends to be slighted in congressional calcula-
tion is the need for executive privacy when such privacy is
designed merely to shield administrative deliberations from
unnecessary or premature publicity. However, since the president can, when he chooses, protect the confidential character
of executive communications from legislative curiosity, the
congressional disinclination to respect executive privacy may
actually be regarded as a useful part of the check-and-balance
system. It certainly acts as a deterrent to any executive tendency to use privacy merely for the purpose of covering up
blunders or to engage in self-serving publicity. In playing this
watchdog role, Congress undoubtedly engages in far more
alarms and excursions than the danger warrants, but this is
the price that society has traditionally had to pay for the
watchdog function.

In spite of the real contribution Congress has made to the
development of administrative secrecy, and indeed the secretive practices it has itself engaged in, the legislature has always
been primarily identified with the cause of publicity in government. For a representative body is, intrinsically, an organ
of publicity which ventilates grievances, exposes malfeasance
on the part of executive officials, and constantly informs itself
and the community of emergent issues in public policy. It is
to the executive rather than the legislature that secrecy comes
most naturally, for, as noted long ago in the *Federalist*, the
executive's capacity for secretive operations is one of its most
enduring assets as a governmental institution. It should not,
therefore, come as any surprise that the trend toward secrecy
in government today owes so large a debt to presidential action and initiative. It is to this subject that we now turn.

[32] See, for example, Harold P. Green, "Atomic Energy Information Control," *Chicago Bar Record*, Vol. 38 (November, 1956), pp. 55–62.

CHAPTER 4

PRESIDENTIAL POWER

THE POWER OF executive agencies to withhold information from the public, the press, and even on occasion from the legislature itself does not rest upon congressional pleasure alone. Quite apart from any specific statutory protection that may exist for the practice of secrecy in administration, judicial decisions long ago established certain common-law privileges which executive agencies may assert in refusing to reveal information contained in government files.[1] The exact scope of the common-law privilege against disclosure is subject to some dispute, but there are at least two areas in which it rests upon solid legal foundation.

Military secrets, for example, and indeed all confidential information bearing on military or diplomatic affairs have always been held to be privileged against disclosure even in the absence of a statute bearing on the subject. A similar status has been accorded executive communications which would tend to reveal the identity of individuals supplying information on criminal activity to law enforcement officials. In cases of this kind, the public interest in secrecy has been held to be so

[1] The best discussion of the common-law basis of executive secrecy may be found in annotation, *United States* ex rel. *Touhy* v. *Ragen*, 95L. ed. 427–34.

essential as to override any contrary claims. Disclosure of military or diplomatic secrets would jeopardize the safety of the state, while the protection afforded confidential informants to the police is regarded as indispensable for effective law enforcement.

There is some judicial indication that internal communications among executive officials also enjoy this common-law privilege against disclosure and that an administrator may invoke this privilege at his own discretion. It has been held, for example, that "communications in writing passing between officers of the government, in the course of official duty, relating to the business of their offices, are privileged from disclosure, on the ground of public policy, and the production will not be compelled by courts of law or equity." [2] In other cases, however, this ruling has not been firmly upheld, and there are outstanding exceptions to it.

Executive Discretion

Ultimately, the power of executive agencies to withhold information in the absence of a statute bearing on the subject stems from the authority of the president himself rather than any common-law privilege. The argument here has been that the president has certain independent constitutional duties to discharge, including the obligation to "take care that the laws be faithfully executed," which entitle him to the privilege of withholding information if he considers that its disclosure would be harmful.[3] And presidents have, on frequent occa-

---

[2] *Gardner* v. *Anderson*, Fed. Cas. No. 5220 (C.C., Dist. Md. 1876), as quoted *ibid.*, p. 433.

[3] For general discussions of presidential control over the release of information, see Edward S. Corwin, *The President, Office and Powers* (N.Y., 1957), pp. 110-17; Glendon A. Schubert, Jr., *The Presidency in the Courts* (Minneapolis, 1957), pp. 327-31.

sion, regarded demands for information as encroachments
upon their legal authority, as well as obstacles to the effective
discharge of their executive responsibilities.

The principle of executive privilege with respect to the release of information was first spelled out during Washington's
administration in response to a request from Congress for
documents related to the ill-fated expedition against the In-
dians led by General St. Clair. In Washington's own words:

> . . . the Executive ought to communicate such papers as the
> public good would permit, and ought to refuse those, the dis-
> closure of which would injure the public: consequently were to
> exercise a discretion.[4]

In this instance it was discovered that no papers requiring
confidential treatment were involved, and the documents requested were eventually sent along to Congress. But in a later
case involving a request from the House for documents connected with the negotiation of the Jay treaty, Washington
refused to comply with a congressional demand for information.

In the years that followed, many other presidents had occasion to restate the principle of executive privacy that Washington had first enunciated. During Jefferson's term of office, the House asked for documents in executive files on the
Burr conspiracy. Jefferson's rejection of this request has a
peculiarly modern ring, resembling, as it does, the recent presidential refusals to release confidential information in FBI
files. Regarding the material that he held with respect to Burr's
alleged efforts to stir up rebellion, Jefferson wrote:

> It is chiefly in the form of letters, often containing such a mixture
> of rumors, conjectures, and suspicions as renders it difficult to

[4] As quoted in *The Power of the President to Withhold Information from
the Congress*, Memorandums of the Attorney-General, Compiled by the Subcommittee on Constitutional Rights of the Senate Committee on the Judiciary,
85th Cong., 2d sess., Feb. 6, 1958, p. 5.

sift out the real facts and unadvisable to hazard more than general outlines, strengthened by concurrent information or the particular credibility of the relator. In this state of the evidence, delivered sometimes, too, under the restriction of private confidence, neither safety nor justice will permit the exposing names. . . .[5]

Jefferson subsequently had the opportunity during Burr's trial to inform John Marshall that presidential papers enjoyed a similar immunity from judicial inspection.

Since Jefferson's day, hardly a decade has gone by when presidents have not refused congressional requests for information. In a great majority of cases, the issue arose as a result of congressional investigation of executive personnel—an area that has been a productive source of discord down to the present time. The incidence of overt conflict in this area has climbed markedly in recent years. According to a tabulation submitted to Congress by the Attorney General in 1957, only 18 instances of dispute between president and Congress over the availability of executive files are recorded prior to 1940. However, in the period since that time, President Truman alone was involved in 15 major incidents of this kind between 1948 and 1952—most of which grew out of congressional efforts to look at FBI files. As noted in the Attorney General's study of this subject:

> An examination of the history of congressional demands upon the Executive for confidential documents during the past 6 years discloses that more has been said in Congress and the press during this period than in the preceding 60 years. Not since the famous debate in the first administration of President Cleveland, in 1886, has there been such extensive public discussion of this question.[6]

[5] *Ibid.*, Feb. 6, 1958, p. 6.
[6] *Ibid.*, Oct. 31, 1958, p. 90.

The fact that recent years have seen such repeated efforts by congressmen and congressional committees to secure access to executive records, even in the face of continued presidential refusals to comply with these requests, gives rise to the suspicion that Congress has come to view this particular terrain as a battleground on which it wins even when it loses. The legislature has not as yet discovered any legal way in which it can force executive officials to reveal matters they refuse to disclose, but it may well have concluded that it wins important ground before the bar of public opinion merely by skirmishing with the president on this issue.

This is not to say the president loses significantly in public esteem when he takes what some may regard as the executive equivalent of the fifth amendment in refusing to open his records to public inspection. No impressive evidence exists that the public thinks less of its presidents for defending the privacy of their files. Indeed, the standing some chief executives have acquired as "strong presidents" may be due in good part to their firmness in resisting acts of apparent legislative usurpation. The bold assertion of "executive privilege" may enhance their standing in the public eye.

But from the viewpoint of the legislator, the important fact is that a joust with the president on this issue offers a heaven-sent opportunity to escape the comparative anonymity of legislative life and to be seen, even if only momentarily, upon the center stage of American politics under the spotlight focused on the decision, activities, and even vagaries of the executive office of the president. Being spurned by a president may not be the best way in which to gain public attention, but for some politicians, it may be better than the obscurity that is the alternative.

Another reason why conflicts over this issue may have special appeal for the congressman is the fact that a president who refuses to disclose information protects his executive privilege of privacy only at the cost of giving some credence to the congressional allegations that have led to a demand for inspection of executive files. Rumors stirred by congressional charges can hardly be laid to rest by presidential secrecy, since secrecy is conducive to the mushroom growth of rumor, as is suggested by the experience of highly secretive societies like the Soviet Union, where rumor substitutes for fact as the ordinary grist of everyday conversation on political matters.[7]

Presidents are here confronted with a Hobson's choice in any event. If, in the interest of dispelling unfounded suspicions, they do yield to requests for disclosure, they may diminish their own standing in the eyes of subordinates, as well as establish a precedent which will multiply congressional demands for information in the future. And they may incur these disadvantages without necessarily disproving the legislative allegations that brought about the disclosure, since executive files will always contain at least some material supporting conclusions contrary to those of the president on, for example, matters of loyalty-security investigations.

But presidents have nonetheless stood firm in defense of the principle of executive independence of dictation by Congress —or, for that matter, the judiciary—on matters they consider to lie within the sphere of their constitutional authority. Even Presidents like William Howard Taft and Calvin Coolidge, notorious for the restrained view they took of presidential power, refused to concede that it lies within the authority of the legislature to compel the disclosure of information the executive feels it necessary to conceal. Taft, for example, noted that

The President is required by the Constitution from time to time to give to Congress information on the state of the Union,

[7] See Douglass Cater, *The Fourth Branch of Government* (Boston, 1959), pp. 188–89.

and to recommend for its consideration such measures as he shall judge necessary and expedient, but this does not enable Congress or either House of Congress to elicit from him confidential information which he has acquired for the purpose of enabling him to discharge his constitutional duties, if he does not deem the disclosure of such information prudent or in the public interest.[8]

For a President chiefly identified historically as a weak rather than a strong President, Taft's "prudent or in the public interest" standard for withholding information stakes out a very broad claim of executive privilege. It lacks some of the fire but none of the breadth of Theodore Roosevelt's dictum delivered while refusing a senatorial demand for information: "heads of the executive departments are subject to the Constitution, and to the laws passed by the Congress in pursuance of the Constitution, and to the directions of the President of the United States, but to no other direction whatever." [9]

The Control of Information

There are varied avenues open to a chief executive wishing to prevent the release of information by executive agencies. In the past, demands for information were often made of the president himself. At issue in the Jefferson administration, for example, was a personal letter to the President from General Wilkinson, an item of correspondence that Burr sought to have produced in court as part of his effort to disprove the charge of treason that had been brought against him. Similarly in Jackson's administration, the Senate sought access to a statement that the President had reportedly read to the

[8] William Howard Taft, *Our Chief Magistrate and His Powers* (N.Y. 1925), p. 129.
[9] As quoted in the study prepared by the Senate Subcommittee on Constitutional Rights, *op. cit.*, p. 17.

heads of the executive departments. Presidents have generally regarded demands of this kind as an invasion of their personal prerogatives as chief executive.

More recently, however, the vast expansion in the size and complexity of the national government has produced a situation in which demands for information are chiefly made of the executive bureaucracy—members of the president's official family or subordinate officials more immediately involved in the day-to-day affairs of administration. In situations of this kind, the question of presidential control over information largely turns on the ability of the chief executive to insure that his subordinates are not compelled to release information that he feels should be kept secret.

As indicated in the previous chapter, there are a great many cases where subordinate officials can defend the privacy of their records by reference to statutes enacted by the legislature itself. These statutes provide wide protection against the release of information to members of the public who may, for example, request its production in connection with litigation in which they are involved. Actually, however, these laws do not provide a firm basis for refusing to disclose information to Congress itself, since it cannot be assumed that the legislature inhibits its own power of inquiry when it enacts laws barring the public from inspecting executive records.

When an executive official does claim the protection of statute in refusing to disclose information, Congress can change the law so as to allow the release of the data it requests. In 1947, for example, the Secretary of Agriculture refused to supply a congressional committee with the names of traders on the commodity market on the ground that he was forbidden to do so by the Commodity Exchange Act. Congress thereupon passed a joint resolution authorizing the Secretary to release the information to the committee that had requested it.[10] However, this case provides precedent for the belief that a law enjoining executive secrecy can be altered only by action of the full legislative body and not by order of a single congressman or committee.

Ultimately, administrative agencies may have to base their refusal to supply Congress with information upon executive authority rather than statute. The president may assert the right, as he has done on notable occasions in the past, to prohibit executive officials from disclosing certain kinds of information without his express permission. This directive may be oral or written, and it may bar all agencies from disclosing certain kinds of information or it may be addressed to a single agency or official.

One example of a general directive is the order issued by President Truman on March 15, 1948, barring the disclosure of information in the executive files on the loyalty of federal employees. This general directive was later supplemented by specific presidential support for a number of refusals by individual executive agencies to supply such information to congressional committees. In this instance a policy of nondisclosure may have been necessary to prevent the demoralization of the civil service, since congressional demands for information were far-reaching, and included demands to know the identity of those who sat on loyalty boards as well as a record of how they voted on cases that came before them. But the Truman policy nonetheless played into the hands of legislators who wanted to arouse suspicion of the effectiveness of the loyalty program, since it eliminated whatever possibility there was of disproving their charges. Senator McCarthy, for example, informed his colleagues that while he had no evidence to support his accusation of disloyalty against eighty-one State Department employees, "the evidence to support the charges

[10] See *Congressional Record*, vol. 93, Part 9, pp. 11612–621.

concerning these individuals would be found in the loyalty files maintained in the executive branch of the government." [11]

Both Truman and Eisenhower had occasion to defend the privacy of communications between themselves and their subordinates when these conversations were preliminary to presidential decisions. Perhaps the most famous incident of this kind occurred during the Truman administration when General Omar Bradley, the Chairman of the Joint Chiefs of Staff, refused to supply a Senate committee with details on conversations that had taken place between the President and his military advisers prior to the removal of General MacArthur from his Far Eastern command. Senator Russell, the chairman of the committee, eventually upheld the legitimacy of this refusal in a ruling that was supported by a majority of his colleagues. This was not the first time that Congress itself had upheld the wisdom of an executive refusal to supply information to the legislature.

On May 17, 1954, President Eisenhower sent a letter to Secretary of Defense Charles Wilson instructing him that neither he nor his subordinates were to testify regarding internal discussions within the executive branch relating to the Army-McCarthy dispute, then under investigation by the Senate Committee on Government Operations. As Eisenhower put it:

> . . . it is essential to efficient and effective administration that employees of the executive branch be in a position to be completely candid in advising with each other on official matters . . . and it is not in the public interest that any of their conversations or communications, or any documents or reproductions, concerning such advice be disclosed. . . .[12]

[11] Senate Subcommittee on Constitutional Rights, *op. cit.*, p. 106.
[12] The Eisenhower letter is reproduced in the *Twenty-Fifth Intermediate Report of the Committee on Government Operations*, 84th Cong., 2d. sess., House Report No. 2947, July 27, 1956, pp. 64–65. President Kennedy, at his

Subsequently, Eisenhower had occasion to extend the scope of executive privacy to include communications to the President from private citizens as well as his subordinates. Rumor circulated in 1958 that the Gaither report on national defense, which had been prepared by a group of distinguished private citizens, was highly critical of certain weaknesses in the nation's military posture, and there were immediate demands for its release to the public. In refusing to accede to these requests, President Eisenhower noted that the willingness of private citizens to volunteer advice to the government was in good part dependent upon the assurance that they would not thereafter be subject to political attack for having expressed their honest opinion.

While the right of a president to maintain the privacy of communications addressed to him personally has met with some question, even more serious objection has been registered to giving all executive agencies the general right to withhold communications from private sources. This issue arose recently in connection with the activities of advisory committees—groups of private citizens who serve a wide variety of executive agencies on a consultative basis. The point was made that the members of many of these committees are in a position to derive benefits from the decisions reached in their deliberations, through, for example, market speculation based on pending changes in official policy. Many of these changes may in fact be based on the recommendations of advisory committees. It was the possible interest of committee members in their own recommendations that led the Moss Subcommittee on Government Information to suggest that the proceedings of these

---

first press conference following his inauguration, indicated a similar determination to withhold information if this should prove necessary. "I must say," Kennedy stated, "that I do not hold the view that all matters and all information which is available to the Executive should be made available at all times [to the public]." *New York Times,* Jan. 26, 1961, p. 10.

administrative bodies be given the widest possible publicity.[13]

It is not always remembered that the privilege of withholding confidential information stems from presidential authority and is not the intrinsic right of each and every administrative agency within the executive establishment. The Civil Service Commission, for example, in at least its initial response to a congressional inquiry regarding the legal basis for its refusal to supply information to the legislature, announced that as part of the executive branch of government it had an inherent right to withhold information from Congress. This assertion of executive privilege on the part of a subordinate agency met with quick congressional challenge, and the Commission was eventually forced to back away from this extravagant claim.[14]

As might be expected, executive agencies have a general tendency to construe their power to withhold information much more broadly than the strict letter of the law would support. It was noted in the previous chapter that the power vested in the heads of executive departments allowing them to control the "custody, use, and preservation" of their records was widely interpreted as legitimizing executive secrecy, even though the legislature only intended to permit executive agencies to institute rules and regulations for the orderly control of information. And President Eisenhower's letter of May 17, 1954, enjoining the secrecy of internal communications regarding the Army-McCarthy dispute was addressed to the Department of Defense, but it was picked up and used by nineteen other executive agencies to justify the secrecy of their own internal deliberations. As we shall see, this tendency of subordinate officials to overextend the legitimate bounds of

---

[13] *Ibid.*, p. 92. See also James R. Wiggins, *Freedom or Secrecy* (N.Y., 1956), pp. 80–82.

[14] See, *Hearings,* House Subcommittee on Government Information, 84th Cong., 1st sess., Nov. 8, 9, and 10, 1955, pp. 397–99.

executive secrecy has been a particular problem in the case of
information affecting national defense or security.

The Classification System

While the flow of confidential information concerning internal executive affairs has been largely controlled by written
directives and oral communications from the president's office,
executive efforts to preserve the security of military and defense information have taken a more formal turn. The most
significant action taken by a president during the past decade
to prevent state secrets from being disclosed was Executive
Order 10–501, entitled "Safeguarding Official Information in
the Interests of the Defense of the United States," which was
issued by President Eisenhower on November 6, 1953. This
order served to establish a very comprehensive system of classifying information that might be of benefit to a potential national adversary and withholding it from public disclosure. It
supplanted Executive Order 10–290, issued by President Truman on September 24, 1951, which had governed the handling
of classified data up to that time.

This new rule was ostensibly designed to widen the flow of
official information to the public. As stated in the press release
accompanying Eisenhower's action, "the order will make it
possible for our citizens to know more of what their government is doing . . . the danger of misuse of the order to ham-
per freedom of information, so vital to the preservation of our
form of government, is minimized." [15] The features of the new
order that were designed to achieve this result included a reduction in the number of agencies entitled to classify information, the elimination of the category of "restricted" informa-

[15] See *Press Release*, The White House, Nov. 6, 1953.

tion (the new system provides for only three categories of classified information: top secret, secret and confidential), and the establishment of procedures for declassifying documents that no longer need to be kept secret.

However, in spite of its intent, this order, like all previous efforts to control the dissemination of official information, has come under heavy attack. This criticism rests partly on the charge that the Eisenhower order, like the Truman directive which preceded it, tends to keep a great deal more information secret than common sense or the national security requires. Congressman Moss, for example, from his vantage point as chairman of the House Subcommittee on Government Information, has made much of the fact that enterprising bureaucrats, have acted under the authority of Executive Order 10–501 in attempting to conceal information on such topics as the use of the bow and arrow in modern warfare and the telephone number from which an official weather forecast may be obtained from the Pentagon.[16] Much of the material that had previously been classified "restricted" was, with the elimination of this category, up-graded into the confidential classification, and many other documents were given a wholly new label, such as "for official use only."

In addition to the rather ludicrous examples that can always be uncovered of bureaucratic timidity in the classification of documents, the quantity of information withheld under any classification system is vast in scope. In 1957 former Assistant Secretary of Defense Charles A. Coolidge testified before the Moss subcommittee that official records were currently being classified at a higher rate than during World War II, when 6 billion documents were given the secrecy label. And in 1960 the Moss subcommittee itself estimated that the Pentagon was

---

[16] For these and other examples of overclassification, see *Twenty-Seventh Report by the Committee on Government Operations*, 85th Cong., 2d sess., House Report No. 1884, June 16, 1958.

wielding secrecy stamps at a rate which created each week a stack of classified documents higher than the Empire State building. In a system geared to protecting security in this way, a tendency develops to interpret security as broadly as possible, and "playing it safe" demands that in doubtful cases a document be given the highest possible classification that it can, by any stretch of the imagination, be awarded. Consequently, overclassification is an almost inevitable cost of any system of withholding defense information.

Of course, some of this overclassification may not be altogether an innocent product of bureaucratic zeal or caution. For an administrator willing to make use of it in this way (although the regulations specifically prohibit its employment for this purpose), the classification system affords an ideal opportunity for withholding information when its release might merely be a source of embarrassment to a defense agency, such as the celebrated case in which the Navy censored a picture of one of its blimps standing on its nose after an abortive landing. Information units within each of the services have a special interest in preventing the release of information that might blur the favorable image they are attempting to present to the public of what their branch of the armed forces is doing, in view of the adverse effect such publicity might have upon recruitment or appropriations.

The fact that the classification system can be used to cover up administrative blunders is not its only disadvantageous aspect from the point of view of a working democracy, for it may also operate as a serious barrier to public appraisal of current trends in official policy. For example, the classification stamp has been used to conceal serious disagreements among professional military officers regarding the adequacy of prevailing defense strategy. When General Matthew Ridgeway was retiring as Army Chief of Staff, his letter vigorously protesting against a cutback in the strength of the Army was given the classification top-secret by the Defense Department, thus precluding, at least temporarily, public awareness and judgment of a dispute then raging within the Defense Department over military strategy in the cold war.

This problem might be more serious were it not for the fact that military officials have been able to bring most disputes into public view through the device of "leaks" to the press. The service which loses out in policy disputes within the inner councils of the executive has been able to muster congressional and public support for its views by ignoring such barriers as may exist on public disclosure of dissent within official circles. Of course the military official who engages in this practice runs some risk. The widely publicized court-martial in 1957 of one army official, Colonel Nickerson, came about as a result of his violation of classification restrictions in precisely this kind of situation. The Secretary of Defense had issued a directive giving the Air Force jurisdiction over 1,500-mile land-based intermediate range ballistic missiles, thus stripping the Army of control over its 1,500-mile Jupiter missile. Nickerson removed classified material from official files and wrote a memorandum criticizing this decision. The Army later discovered that this document had been circulated among a variety of individuals outside the government, including a newspaper columnist and a magazine editor.

There have been several official studies of the classification system, such as that undertaken by a five-man committee headed by Charles Coolidge, which was appointed by the Secretary of Defense in 1957. These studies have generally concentrated upon tightening the system so as to prevent unauthorized leaks of official information. As noted in the previous chapter, the most effective way in which this can be accomplished is through the establishment of a system under which newspapermen who write stories based on leaks can be forced to disclose their sources of information. The appointment of the Coolidge committee followed shortly after the publication of articles in the *New York Times* outlining points at issue within the armed services over defense policy, including one serious dispute over a proposal to cut the armed forces by 800,000 men. When it turned in its report, the committee recommended that the authors of newspaper stories containing classified information be required to appear and identify their sources before a grand jury—a procedure which would have enabled the Secretary of Defense to take disciplinary action against informants. This recommendation was not, however, accepted by the Secretary.[17]

As the situation now stands, the leak often serves as something of a safety valve against the practice of using the classification system to cover up mistakes, or to prevent public knowledge of serious disagreement over matters of policy. The operation of the present system is thus based upon a process of compensating errors. The error of overclassification is counter-balanced by the error of leaks, and in a good many cases it may be assumed that these errors effectively cancel each other out. However, this cancellation effect cannot be taken for granted, for it is at least equally plausible that there will be cases in which the errors will in fact be cumulative, and that defense policy will simultaneously suffer from both inadequate and excessive resort to the classification system. Moreover, to rely upon leaks is in the last analysis to depend upon fortuitous accidents for the availability of information.

Neither the Coolidge committee nor any other study of secrecy in national defense has been able to devise a system for preventing overclassification. All such attempts have foundered on the fact that the penalties attached to the release of information which injures the national security must necessarily be

---

[17] The report of the Coolidge Committee may be found in *Hearings*, House Subcommittee on Government Information, 85 Cong., 1st sess., March 11, 12, 1957, pp. 2133–46.

made more severe than those associated with the practice of giving a document a higher security classification than it deserves. To be sure the argument can always be made that excessive classification may itself be detrimental to national defense, since, as noted before, both scientific and technological development may be grievously handicapped by barriers to the free flow of information. But this consideration cannot be expected to have anywhere near as sharp an impact upon administrative behavior as the threat of legal sanctions that may swiftly follow upon the unauthorized disclosure of state secrets.

There is another characteristic of the classification system which provides a built-in psychological inducement toward excessive secrecy. This is the fact that the official who originates a document has traditionally had a large voice in determining its final classification. Under this system the administrators involved have a vested interest in giving their material the highest possible security classification, since the "top-secret" label enhances the importance of the document that is being classified and, an official may well assume, the status of its author. In the light of one authoritative estimate that over one-million persons are now involved in the process of classifying documents in the federal civil service, the potential impact of psychological inducements to overclassification is obvious, and it has led to proposals for cutting back sharply on the number of persons entitled to put the classification stamp upon executive records. Under congressional pressure the number of agencies entitled to classify documents has been greatly reduced in recent years.

Excessive classification also tends to weaken respect for the entire system of withholding defense information. When the files are full of trivial material that has been given classified status, a tendency develops to regard the entire classification system with contempt. This point was made with telling force by the Coolidge committee:

. . . the system has become so overloaded that proper protection of information which should be protected has suffered. The press regards the stamp of classification with feelings which vary from indifference to active contempt. Within the Department of Defense itself the mass of classified papers has inevitably resulted in a casual attitude toward classified information, at least on the part of many.[18]

One of the real problems in this regard is the timing of classification. A good many documents may need to be kept secret at the time they are classified, but they tend to retain this status long after there is any need for secrecy regarding their contents.

The obvious solution for this problem is of course, to develop an effective system for declassifying documents once secrecy has outlived its usefulness. Executive Order 10–501 contained a provision for setting a time limit on classification, but this provision was not given effective enforcement until very recently, when in 1960 the Pentagon issued a directive providing for an automatic process of declassification over a twelve-year period. Even then, however, critics noted that the list of subjects exempted from the declassification scheme exceeded those that were included in it. The basic problem here is that declassification is itself handicapped by the same set of psychological factors that have led to the problem it is designed to meet:

> Over-classification is seldom criticized and is safe for the individual making the decision. There are no penalties for recommending a level of classification higher than required but severe penalties for underclassifying. Declassification is a serious step, placing the person responsible in a position to be faced with security charges if someone later criticizes his decision.[19]

---

[18] *Ibid.*, p. 2136.
[19] Statement by Dr. M. Stanley Livingston, *Hearings*, House Subcommittee on Government Information, March 7, 8, 9, 1956, p. 730.

Declassification also presents very substantial administrative and physical problems, involving as it does, a re-study of the status of literally millions of documents that have been classified under the present practice of withholding defense information.

The problem of developing adequate limits upon the classification system has been complicated by the fact that defense agencies have introduced prohibitions on disclosure which cover data having, at best, only an indirect relationship to national security. In 1955, for example, the National Security Council issued a directive establishing an Office of Strategic Information in the Department of Commerce. The purpose of this agency was to prevent the dissemination of unclassified information of a scientific, technical, or economic character (by private contractors as well as government agencies) which might be of service to foreign intelligence agencies.[20] The attempts of this agency to control the exchange of unclassified data aroused widespread misgivings, and it was finally abolished in 1958.

The Defense Department has also made an effort to restrict the release of confidential information which is not related to security matters. On March 29, 1955, Secretary of Defense Charles E. Wilson issued a directive stipulating that clearance of Defense Department information should be based in part on whether "release or publication of the material would constitute a constructive contribution to the primary mission of the Department of Defense." Under this directive clearance was refused to material such as an article by a Navy officer on the sinking of the *Indianapolis* during World War II. This decision was taken on the grounds that details of this mishap

---

[20] See *Twenty-Fifth Intermediate Report of the Committee on Government Operations*, 84th Cong., 2d sess., House Report No. 2947, July 27, 1956, pp. 21–27. During this same year the Defense Department also issued a directive advising defense contractors against the release of information that might be "of possible value to a potential enemy."

might prejudice young men against enlisting in the Navy.[21] Like the order setting up the OSI, this directive came under heavy criticism from legislators and newspapermen, and it was repealed in 1958. An interesting sidelight of these incidents is the clear evidence they provide of the effectiveness of Congress and the press as instruments of restraint upon executive secrecy.

Presidential Responsibility

In legal theory as well as practical operation, the American governmental system has always been thoroughly identified with the practice of countervailing power or the familiar pattern of "checks and balances." And yet it is no small paradox that there are critical aspects in which the system can only operate effectively through self-restraint rather than the method of pitting power against power. This is certainly the case with executive secrecy, where legislative and judicial curbs go only part way toward relieving the danger of possible abuse of administrative authority. In the large areas in which there is still ample executive discretion to withhold information, primary reliance must inevitably be placed upon presidential influence to see to it that administrators hold the practice of secrecy within reasonable limits.

In the area of non-defense information, presidents have been quick to assert the need for privacy as essential both for the effectiveness of executive deliberations and the protection of private citizens having confidential business with the government. While these claims are entirely justifiable within proper limits, extreme presidential care is called for to see that these limits are not quickly overrun. Otherwise, executive

[21] See Wallace Parks, "Secrecy and the Public Interest in Military Affairs," *The George Washington Law Review,* Vol. 26 (October, 1957), pp. 69–70.

privacy may easily degenerate into a convenient instrument
for concealing blunders. Dixon-Yates is but one of many illustrations of situations where administrative privacy was used
to cloak improper activity.

And the president needs to remember that the executive
office itself has a sizeable stake in maintaining opportunities
for publicity regarding administrative activities. For with the
vast expansion that has occurred in the size of executive bureaucracy, the task of policing the activities of the countless
array of agencies that now exercise the powers of government
is far too formidable a task to be accomplished by overhead
presidential supervision alone. It demands substantial assistance
from auxiliary agencies of control such as the press and the
legislature, and these auxiliary agencies cannot function effectively if they are constantly met with the claim of executive
privilege when they seek to force government agencies to disclose information concerning their operations.

Moreover, the tasks with which presidential policy-making
today must grapple are so formidable in breadth and complexity as to demand untiring efforts to acquaint the public
with the facts, as a means of dealing with problems such as
civil defense, which demand public co-operation, and of draw-
ing upon the intellectual resources of the community in the
formation of policy in a variety of other areas. This last consideration seldom receives the recognition it deserves—the
extent to which executive policy-making may be the wiser as
a result of public participation in its development.

And it is important to note that the compartmentalization of
knowledge which flows from the system of classifying defense
information may have highly disadvantageous effects even
within the executive branch of government itself. For in large
areas the classification system operates on a "need to know"
criterion which restricts information to those officials who

have a recognized and acknowledged need to receive such data in connection with their work. But the truth of the matter is that it is not always possible to know beforehand the areas of policy or the policy-makers who may benefit from being made aware of classified information. Most policy problems are so wide-ranging in their implications that it is difficult, if not impossible, to identify the areas of information relevant to their solution.

George Kennan, for example, relates that in 1950, while serving as head of the policy planning division of the State Department, he did not know the number of bombs in this country's nuclear stockpile. As Kennan put it: "I have never known the number of our bombs nor the real facts of their destructiveness or any of those things." [22] Here as elsewhere, diplomatic policy is often made in ignorance of military capabilities. And so, while the vitality of internal executive deliberations may be served by secrecy, to the degree that it facilitates the candid expression of opinion without fear of political reprisal, it may also be gravely handicapped by such secrecy, inasmuch as it conceals data on which an informed system of policy-making depends. Recently it was revealed that Secretary of the Navy Forrestal was not informed of this country's agreement with England not to employ atomic weapons without mutual consent "until he was elevated to the position of

[22] U.S. Atomic Energy Commission, *In the Matter of J. Robert Oppenheimer*, Transcript of Hearing before Personnel Security Board, Washington, D.C., April 12, 1954, through May 6, 1954, p. 366. However, upon reading this paragraph, one scholar with wide experience in public affairs commented as follows:

> In my opinion this does not stand up. Kennan could get what he had to have. If he didn't know "the real facts of (their) destructiveness," I am inclined to view this as Kennan's fault, not the system's. Part of the problem, in this particular context, has to do with State itself. At times it has been unrealistic and has not moved to keep up with the logic of the times. Not every mountain has to come to Mohammed. Every now and again Mohammed, himself, ought to take a trip.

Secretary of Defense, and then he was informed of it, not by executive officials, but by . . . two Senators." [23]

The central fact with which all chief executives must now come to terms is that a classification system designed in the short run to protect national security may at the same time choke off the flow of communications essential for scientific development and the long-run interests of national security. While the union between science and warfare in modern society has made executive secrecy increasingly necessary, it has also made it increasingly hazardous. Presidential statesmanship of a high order may be called for in the future if it proves necessary to buy scientific progress at the price of greater disclosure of scientific information. Reliance must be placed upon executive initiative to take this risk, in view of the fact, noted in the previous chapter, that Congress, although predominantly inclined to favor greater publicity in wide areas of executive activity, has tended to give uncritical acceptance to the need for secrecy in matters affecting the national security.

[23] John G. Palfrey, "The Problem of Secrecy," *Annals* of the American Academy of Political and Social Science, Vol. 290 (November 1953), p. 95.

CHAPTER 5

THE COURTS AND SECRECY

THE PROBLEM of administrative secrecy has come before the courts chiefly in connection with litigation in which the production of government records or testimony is requested, and where such demands are met by a government refusal to furnish this evidence on the grounds that it would reveal matters that should not under law or in the public interest be disclosed. In dealing with these claims on the part of executive agencies, the courts have enunciated a variety of rulings, as the circumstances in which the privilege of secrecy is asserted have differed. Cases in which the government has argued that disclosure of information in its hands would jeopardize the national security have been handled by the judiciary in a quite different fashion than have cases in which the privilege of secrecy is claimed for information the government regards as "confidential" though it does not involve state secrets. Moreover, in this latter area of non-security information, the courts have distinguished between cases in which the government is a third party to litigation and cases in which it is itself a direct participant in such proceedings. Other judicial distinctions have been drawn with respect to the kind of official from whom disclosure will be required, as well as the type of information an executive agency can be asked to reveal.[1]

[1] An even more complex pattern of judicial decisions has evolved at the

State Secrets

In general, however, it would be correct to say that the net impact of judicial decision has been highly favorable to the development of practices of secrecy in the operations of executive agencies. This is especially true where material relating to the national security is involved in the government's refusal to disclose information before the courts. As enunciated in several decisions, the judicial view has been that in cases of this kind the safety of the state must take precedence over all conflicting claims. Consequently, the government has been granted what amounts to an absolute privilege against the disclosure of information relating to matters of military or diplomatic significance. The leading case in this area is *Totten* v. *United States*,[2] where the Supreme Court held that a suit against the government could not even be entertained in the Court of Claims if it would inevitably result in the disclosure of a state secret. A contract allegedly entered into by President Lincoln, engaging Totten to carry on espionage activities behind Southern lines in the Civil War was, therefore, beyond inspection in court. Subsequent decisions, though few in number, have similarly upheld the right of executive officials to suppress information affecting national security.[3]

---

state level. See, in this connection, William V. Sanford, "Evidentiary Privileges Against the Production of Data Within the Control of Executive Departments," *Vanderbilt Law Review*, Vol. 3 (1949), pp. 73–98.

[2] 92 U.S. 105 (1876).

[3] See *United States* v. *Haugen*, 58 F. Supp. 436 (1944). "The right of the army to refuse to disclose confidential information, the secrecy of which it deems necessary to national defense, is indisputable." (*id.*, 438). State secrets have also been protected against disclosure in litigation between private parties. See, for example, *In re Grove*, 180 F. 62 (1910), where a defendant was acquitted of contempt for a refusal to divulge state secrets; *Firth Sterling Steel Co.* v. *Bethlehem Steel Co.*, 199 F. 353 (1912), where evidence was stricken from the record on the grounds that it embodied state secrets; and *Pollen* v. *Ford Instrument Co.*, 26 F. Supp. 583 (1939), where the court sus-

Though the rule against disclosure of military and diplomatic information is clear, there are two problems arising in this connection that have occasioned judicial disagreement. The first is the question of whether the government, in claiming the privilege of withholding state secrets from disclosure in litigation in which it is involved, should by that fact be regarded as having conceded that the point of evidence in dispute should be resolved in favor of the adversary party. Are there, in other words, circumstances in which the government must accept defeat in litigation as the price for suppressing state secrets in judicial proceedings? A second and equally controversial problem that has been presented the courts is that of determining whether to examine the documents alleged to contain state secrets, or to withhold this judicial inspection on the grounds that it would itself be a violation of security.[4]

Both of these problems were presented to a district court in the case of *Reynolds* v. *United States*.[5] The crash of an Air Force plane caused the death of three civilian engineers who were aboard the plane for the purpose of testing secret electronics equipment. The widows of those killed brought suit for damages against the government under the Federal Tort Claims Act, and their attorneys requested production of an Air Force investigative report on the accident as well as the

---

tained an objection by a litigant that production of documents requested would represent a violation of the Espionage Act.

Documents contained within the diplomatic files of foreign governments have also been held to be privileged from disclosure in judicial proceedings. See *Kessler* v. *Best*, 121 F. 439 (1903), *Viereck* v. *United States*, 130 F. 2d. 945 (1942). The official claiming this privilege must, however, "make a showing that he is entitled to one." *Crosby* v. *Pacific S.S. Lines*, 133 F. 2d. 470 (1943).

[4] See, in this connection, Robert Haydock, "Evidentiary Problems Posed by Atomic Energy Security Requirements," *Harvard Law Review*, Vol. 61 (1948), pp. 468–91; Dale McAllister, "Executive or Judicial Determination of Privilege of Government Documents?" *Journal of Criminal Law and Criminology*, Vol. 41 (1950), pp. 330–35.

[5] 10 F.R.D. 468 (1950).

statements of surviving crew members. Upon being ordered
by the court to furnish these reports the Attorney-General
and the Secretary of the Air Force refused to comply, for
among other reasons the fact that disclosure of this material
would reveal military secrets. The court then asked that the
documents in question be presented for inspection, in order
that the presiding judge might verify the claim that they included privileged material. Again the government refused the
court's request, and it was then held that, in accordance with
the Federal Rules of Civil Procedure, the issue of negligence
must automatically be decided in favor of the plaintiffs, who
were thereby entitled to damages. This decision was subsequently upheld by the Court of Appeals.[6]

However, when the issue was taken before the Supreme
Court, the judgment was reversed. The Supreme Court ruled
that the government had made a valid claim of privilege, since
there were reasonable grounds for believing that exposure of
the documents in question would have endangered military
secrets.[7] In a case of this kind, the Court declared, a judge is
not warranted in insisting that he be given an opportunity to
inspect personally documents for which the privilege of secrecy is invoked, but should content himself with determining
that, as was true in this case, there is a reasonable possibility
that state secrets are contained in such records. In the Court's
own words, it is sufficient to determine "from all the circumstances of the case, that there is a reasonable danger that com-
pulsion of the evidence will expose military matters which, in
the interest of national security, should not be divulged."

In a dissenting opinion three Supreme Court justices stated
their agreement with the decision by the Court of Appeals
which had sustained judgment in favor of the plaintiffs. The
Court of Appeals had held that the documents in question

---

[6] Reynolds v. United States, 192 F. 2d. 987 (1951).
[7] *United States* v. *Reynolds,* 345 U.S. 1 (1953).

were indispensable for determining the issue of negligence, and that the trial judge should have been given the opportunity to inspect this material *in camera* to see if it contained matters privileged against disclosure. A refusal of the government to allow such inspection had been the procedural equivalent of admission that negligence had in fact occurred, and judgment had, therefore, been rendered correctly in favor of the plaintiffs. Although this view has met with considerable approval,[8] as the matter now stands in civil litigation, the government may invoke the privilege of secrecy in the interest of concealing matters affecting national security without either allowing inspection by the courts of the material for which the privilege is claimed, or accepting defeat in litigation as a result of its suppression of information. It should of course be noted that while the minority view disputes these points, it does not seek to force the government actually to disclose state secrets in a public proceeding.

A perplexing issue is of course posed the courts by an executive agency's claim that material it refuses to reveal contains state secrets. Against a judicial policy of accepting such a claim at face value stands of course the consideration that an executive agency may misuse the power thus granted by classifying as secret documents which might merely be damaging to its case in court. However, serious difficulties confront any policy of judicial inspection aimed at evaluating the accuracy of the government's claim that documents it refuses to disclose contain state secrets. For while judges would be quick to point out that such material would be no less safe in their hands than it would be in the possession of an executive official,[9] the plain

[8] See, for example, Comment, "The Executive Evidential Privilege in Suits Against the Government," *Northwestern University Law Review*, Vol. 47 (1952), pp. 259–69.
[9] See, in this regard, the discussion by Raoul Berger and Abe Krash, "Government Immunity from Discovery," *Yale Law Journal*, Vol. 59 (1950), pp. 1451–66.

fact of the matter is that the security of a state secret is inversely proportional to the number of people who know of its existence, and this fact alone would argue against judicial inspection.

Moreover, there is the additional consideration that judges have no particular competence to determine at what points state secrets are included within documents they may inspect, given the fact that much of this material is highly technical in character. As a result judicial inspection would in the end have to be made in secret under executive guidance. A court inspection conducted *in camera* and controlled by the executive would seem to represent small profit to a private litigant compared to the risk involved to the nation in increasing the number of individuals aware of the existence of a state secret. Of course, from the point of view of a private litigant, an inadequate inspection may be preferable to no inspection at all.

In handing down the Reynolds decision, the court noted that the same rationale might not apply in criminal cases where the government is the moving party in litigation. One of the principal cases in which this issue arose in recent years was *United States* v. *Coplon*,[10] where a circuit court ruled that "there may be evidence—'state secrets'—to divulge which will imperil 'national security'; and which the Government cannot, and should not be required to divulge. *Salus rei publicae suprema lex.*" However, Justice Learned Hand, speaking for the court, also went on to say that the government cannot actually convict anyone of a criminal offense upon the basis of state secrets which it refuses to reveal. On this point Hand was quite firm:

> Few weapons in the arsenal of freedom are more useful than the power to compel a government to disclose the evidence on which it seeks to forfeit the liberty of its citizens. . . . A society which has come to wince at such exposure of the methods by

[10] 185 F. 2d. 629 (1950).

which it seeks to impose its will upon its members, has already
lost the feel of freedom and is on the path toward absolutism.

In cases of this kind the government is faced with what one
observer has called a "truth or consequences" dilemma, forced
to choose between revealing state secrets or allowing a defendant to go free. In this instance the defendant, Judith Coplon, did escape further prosecution for espionage activity even
though, as Hand himself noted, her "guilt is plain."

Confidential Information

Judicial rulings with regard to official or confidential information that executive agencies refuse to disclose are, as has
been suggested, somewhat more complex. In a long line of
decisions the courts have, in the first place, upheld the right
of executive officials to refuse to give testimony or produce
documents in court relating to such confidential data in litigation in which the government is not itself directly involved,
but where the information is sought in connection with a dispute between other parties. The leading case here is *Boske*
v. *Comingore*, in which a local collector of internal revenue
employed by the Treasury Department refused a request by
the State of Kentucky that he produce reports filed with the
department that were needed as evidence in a prosecution
undertaken by the state.[11] The collector was jailed in conse-
quence of this refusal, which was based on a general regulation of the Treasury Department forbidding subordinate employees to disclose information obtained in the course of their
official duties.[12] The Supreme Court, in holding this detention
illegal, enunciated what has since become the guiding formula

---

[11] 177 U.S. 459 (1900).
[12] The order was issued on April 15, 1898, and quoted in full in the decision
of the Court.

in this area of the law. The head of an executive agency may, under the general housekeeping power granted him by Congress, issue regulations controlling "the custody, use and preservation" of documents relating to the work of the department, and a subordinate employee cannot be required to disobey such regulations.

In a variety of rulings subsequently handed down, the courts have followed the precedent set in this early decision. Several of these cases have, like *Boske* v. *Comingore*, dealt with the power of internal revenue officials employed by the Treasury Department to keep tax files closed from public inspection,[13] and the courts have stoutly defended the practice of secrecy in this area of administration. However, the right of other executive agencies to resort to the same privilege has also been upheld.[14] One issue in this area has not as yet been entirely clarified by the courts. The cases to date deal with situations in which a subordinate administrator, acting under orders from

[13] See *In re Lamberton*, 124 Fed. 446 (1903), *Stegall* v. *Thurman*, 175 Fed. 813 (1010). Earlier cases in which a similar decision was rendered include *In re Huttman*, 70 Fed. 699 (1895), and *In re Weeks*, 82 Fed. 729 (1897). An apparent exception, *In re Hirsch*, 74 Fed. 928 (1896) was overruled by *Boske* v. *Comingore*. In these cases the courts have protected both the secrecy of tax records and the refusal of revenue officials to give information obtained by them in their official capacities. In this area of tax administration, the issue arises mainly in connection with prosecutions under state law at which the testimony of national officials is requested. The same privilege of secrecy has been accorded tax officials at the state level. See *In Re Valecia Condensed Milk Co.*, 240 Fed. 310 (1917).

[14] *Ex Parte Sackett*, 74 F. 2d 922 (1935). In *Harris* v. *Walsh*, 277 Fed. 569 (1922) and *Federal Life Insurance Co.* v. *Holod*, 30 F. Supp. 713 (1940), the secrecy of selective service records was also protected by the courts from disclosure. See also *Harwood* v. *McMurty*, 22 F. Supp. 572 (1938), *United States* ex rel. *Bayarsky* v. *Brooks*, 51 F. Supp. 974 (1943), and *Universal Air Lines* v. *Eastern Air Lines*, 188 F. 2d 993 (1951). The privilege of secrecy must, however, be invoked by the government official qualified to do so. See *Zimmerman* v. *Poindexter*, 74 F. Supp. 933 (1947). In *FTC* v. *Dilger*, 276 F. 2d 739 (1960), a Court of Appeals decision which the Supreme Court subsequently refused to review, the secrecy of a report to the Census Bureau was protected even against the attempt of another government agency—the Federal Trade Commission—to have it disclosed.

his administrative superior, refuses a request for the disclosure of confidential information. However, in a case decided in 1951, *Touhy* v. *Ragen*,[15] the Supreme Court intimated that if a litigant were to be successful in having a court order served on the executive official from whose authority the regulations requiring secrecy is actually derived, the precedent of *Boske* v. *Comingore* might not apply.[16]

Touhy v. *Ragen* thus pointed up a fundamental ambiguity in this area of the law. Past decisions have accepted the fact that the head of an executive agency can retain control over so important an area of decision-making as the release of confidential information to the public, and that he can, therefore, withdraw discretion from his subordinates in this as in other areas of policy.[17] However, the courts have not as yet specifically ruled on the extent to which a departmental executive himself has the power to suppress information from public disclosure in this type of case; it has merely accepted his right to remove this power from others. In an opinion concurring with the decision in *Touhy* v. *Ragen*, Justice Frankfurter indicated his belief that precedents in this area by no means foreclose the possibility that a future court may demand of the head of an executive agency that he produce documents relevant to litigation before it. As Frankfurter put it: "To hold now that the Attorney-General is empowered to forbid his subordinates, though within the court's jurisdiction, to produce documents and to hold later that the Attorney-General him-

[15] *United States* ex rel. *Touhy* v. *Ragen et al.*, 340 U.S. 462 (1951).

[16] *Ibid.*, 464. "The constitutionality of the Attorney General's exercise of a determinative power as to whether or on what conditions or subject to what disadvantages to the Government he may refuse to produce government papers under his charge, must await a factual situation that requires a ruling."

[17] As stated in *Touhy* v. *Ragen*, 482: "When one considers the variety of information contained in the files of any government department and the possibilities of harm from unrestricted disclosure in court, the usefulness, indeed the necessity of centralizing determination as to whether *subpoenas duces tecum* will be willingly obeyed or challenged is obvious."

self cannot in any event be procedurally reached would be to apply a fox-hunting theory of justice that ought to make Bentham's skeleton rattle." However, since there are in most cases of this kind substantial procedural difficulties involved in serving a court order upon the head of an executive agency,[18] the extent of administrative secrecy which is protected under the Boske ruling is still very broad, whatever untoward effect this may have upon Bentham's skeleton.

In cases in which the government is a direct party to litigation, the courts have not usually been as willing to grant executive officials the same latitude in suppressing information regarded as confidential as they have when the government is merely a third party to proceedings before the court. In, for example, criminal prosecutions instituted by executive agencies, the courts have in a number of decisions established the same rule which prevails in cases involving state secrets. The government cannot refuse to disclose confidential information relevant to a criminal trial without at the same time allowing the defendant to go free. Justice Learned Hand's opinion in *United States* v. *Andolschek* is often quoted: "While we must accept it as lawful for a department of the government to suppress documents, even when they will help determine controversies between third persons, we cannot agree that this should include their suppression in a criminal prosecution, founded upon those very dealings to which the documents relate, and whose criminality they will, or may, tend to exculpate. . . . The government must choose; either it must leave the transactions in the obscurity from which a trial will draw them, or it must expose them fully."[19]

The one exception to this general rule arises in connection

[18] These difficulties are discussed in Note, "The Touhy Case: The Governmental Privilege to Withhold Documents in Private Litigation," *Northwestern University Law Review*, Vol. 47 (1952), pp. 519–30.

[19] 142 F. 2d 503 (1944). See also *United States* v. *Beekman*, 155 F. 2d 580 (1946), *United States* ex rel. *Schleuter* v. *Watkins*, 67 F. Supp. 556 (1946), *United States* v. *Grayson*, 166 F. 2d 863 (1948).

with requests for information that would lead to disclosure of the identity of confidential informants to law enforcement agencies. The courts have been unswerving in their conviction that an effective law enforcement system demands that the names of those who supply information concerning illegal activities can, if the government chooses, be kept secret. Consequently, even in criminal proceedings, requests for information that would expose the identity of such informants have been uniformly denied.

The privilege of secrecy also applies to the information supplied by these confidential informants. This policy adheres to an early ruling of the Supreme Court to the effect that "such information, given by a private citizen, is a privileged and confidential communication, for which no action of libel and slander will lie, and the disclosure of which cannot be compelled without the assent of the government." [20] However, the prosecution loses the privilege of suppressing confidential evidence when it calls the source of that information to testify.[21] This is an old principle which (as noted in Chapter 3) caused such widespread apprehension when it was reaffirmed in *Jencks* v. *United States.*

The courts have also protected the anonymity of confidential informants in civil cases. In the field of antitrust, for example, it has been held that "the considerations which require the withholding of information and its source from the accused by the Government in criminal cases are present also in civil and antitrust actions brought for the public interest by the Government." [22]

[20] *In re Quarles*, 158 U.S. 532 (1895). See also *Vogel* v. *Gruaz*, 110 U.S. 311 (1884); *Arnstein* v. *United States*, 296 F. 946 (1924); *Scher* v. *United States*, 95 F. 2d 64, 305 U.S. 251 (1938); *United States* v. *Ebeling*, 146 F. 2d 254 (1944).

[21] See *United States* v. *Krulewitch*, 145 F. 2d 76 (1944). This problem is discussed in Richard C. Donnelly, "Judicial Control of Informants, Spies, Stool Pigeons, and Agent Provocateurs," *Yale Law Journal*, Vol. 60 (1951), pp. 1091–1131.

[22] *United States* v. *Deere & Co.*, 9 F.R.D. 523 (1949).

Otherwise, however, the government has been denied the right to withhold information in the case of civil actions which it initiates. The rationale here as stated by one judge is that it would be unfair to allow a situation to develop in which "one party may obtain evidence from another, upon which it seeks an injunction of wide application and to hold the latter in liability for a large penalty, and may refuse to reveal that evidence where required by orderly procedure in the suit brought, on the claim that it is confidential." [23] In civil as in criminal cases it is of course necessary for the defendant to show that the information it seeks from the government is relevant to the subject matter of the case. The right of a defendant to obtain pertinent information from the government does not comprehend the right to engage in a "fishing expedition" into government files. Unless some showing of "good cause" for disclosure is required, the task of complying with demands for information might take up a good deal of the time and energy of executive officials.[24]

Where the government holds the status of defendant in a civil action brought by a private party, it has under judicial decision also been refused the right to withhold inspection of material it classifies as confidential information.[25] The courts have here reasoned that where the government consents to be sued, it does so, unless otherwise specified, upon the understanding that it will be treated no differently than a private litigant, and it must, therefore, submit to the discovery of evi-

---

[23] *Bowles* v. *Ackerman*, 4 F.R.D. 260 (1945). See also *Fleming* v. *Bernardi*, 4 F.R.D. 270 (1941); *United States* v. *Cotton Valley Operators Committee*, 9 F.R.D. 719 (1949); affirmed *per curiam* 339 U.S. 940 (1950); *Walling* v. *Richmond Screw Anchor Co.*, 4 F.R.D. 265 (1943). For an exception, see, however, *Walling* v. *Comet Carriers, Inc.*, 3 F.R.D. 442 (1944).

[24] See *Alltmont* v. *United States*, 177 F. 2d 971 (1949); *Bowman Dairy Co.* v. *United States*, 341 U.S. 214 (1951).

[25] See *Cresmer* v. *United States*, 9 F.R.D. 203 (1949); *Bank Line* v. *United States*, 76 F. Supp. 801 (1948); *O'Neill* v. *United States*, 79 F. Supp. 827 (1948); *Evans* v. *United States*, 10 F.R.D. 255 (1950).

dence within its possession. This rule applies, of course, only in
situations where the government invokes the privilege of secrecy in the interest of concealing confidential information.
Under the Reynolds decision, as previously discussed, an executive agency still retains the right to refuse to divulge information in civil litigation in which it is a defendant if the
material requested relates to military or diplomatic secrets.

In summary, therefore, it is clear that the rules developed
by the judiciary in connection with litigation that has come
before the courts provide ample protection for the practice of
administrative secrecy. This protection is quite extensive in the
area of both state secrets and confidential information. Through
adherence to the precedent of *Boske* v. *Comingore*, the courts
have virtually foreclosed the possibility that sizeable leaks in
administrative secrecy might be sprung through litigation involving other parties in which the disclosure of confidential
information in government files is required. In cases in which
the government is itself directly involved in judicial proceedings, no such immunity from disclosure is allowed, but the
sanction imposed upon an executive agency in this area for a
refusal to reveal information—defeat in litigation—does not
in itself force the disclosure of information it may wish to
conceal. In addition, of course, executive agencies are in every
instance accorded the substantial privilege of refusing to divulge the identity of confidential informants to law enforcement officials. The courts have, therefore, given their blessing
to the practice of administrative secrecy as a matter of public
policy in certain areas, and in other instances have found it
possible to give judicial relief without forcing disclosure of
administrative secrets.

The courts have not yet answered the question of whether
the national legislature, as distinguished from private litigants,
can obtain a legal remedy in its efforts to force executive
agencies to disclose information they decline to reveal. This

dispute has so far been carried on in the arena of politics rather than law. Congress has had great success in obtaining information which it requests from executive officials and records. Its success in this respect can of course be traced to the very telling sanctions the legislature can impose, through, for example, its appropriations and law-making power, upon executive agencies which refuse to co-operate in supplying data requested. An administrative agency risks a great deal in remaining obdurate in opposition to a legislative demand for information, though, as already noted, executive officials have on occasion been willing or obliged to take that risk under presidential directive. If the question does come before the courts, it will be as a result of a contempt citation entered by Congress against an executive official refusing to testify or produce documents claimed as privileged from disclosure in a legislative inquiry.

Privacy and Democracy

For many people the problem of striking a balance between secrecy and disclosure in administration presents none of the difficulty which this complex pattern of judicial distinctions would suggest. Administrative secrecy is on all counts to be abhorred as being a salient characteristic of an authoritarian society and altogether repugnant to the spirit and practice of constitutionalism. Whatever the courts may say, it should, therefore, be held within the narrowest limits consistent with the safety of state secrets it is absolutely necessary to conceal from unfriendly foreign eyes. This is certainly the viewpoint of spokesmen of the media of communications, and, as has already been suggested, this has been the prevailing view in the American political tradition.

Moreover, while many would argue that the fierce hot light

of publicity has on occasion been so blinding as to dim the vision of both the public and its officials, there is no doubt that publicity is indeed a cornerstone of democracy. Public knowledge of the affairs of state is indispensable if the people are in fact as in theory to participate in the governing process, for knowledge is, in this respect at least, power. Otherwise, the capacity of administrative officials to withhold information presents them with the opportunity to conceal mistakes that should be revealed for the purpose of fixing responsibility and rectifying error. Nothing could be more axiomatic for a democracy than the principle of exposing the processes of government to relentless public criticism and scrutiny.

A telling consideration which buttresses the need for adequate publicity is the fact that the communication process goes on even where government officials choose to withhold information. However, in this event public opinion is shaped by rumor rather than accurate information, and the popular judgments consequently formed may be wildly erroneous. This problem is illustrated in recent experience by the Comptroller of the Currency's policy of withholding information on proposed mergers of national banks until the merger has actually been completed. The Comptroller defended this policy before the Moss subcommittee on the grounds that "it would be harmful to all concerned if we announced mergers which had not definitely been agreed upon at least by the directors of the banks concerned. It is harmful to a bank and to its stockholders to have an announcement of merger made, and then have the merger fail to go through." [26]

Representative Moss, however, noted that unwarranted rumors were sometimes spread about pending mergers for, among other reasons, the purpose of stimulating stock prices and that a policy of disclosing information on proposed merg-

[26] See *Hearings*, House Subcommittee on Government Information, 84th Cong., 1st sess., Nov. 8, 9, 10, 1955, pp. 210–11.

ers by the Comptroller could well serve to nip such rumors in the bud.[27] This criticism points up a major problem of administrative secrecy—the fact that it may, in some cases, prevent executive agencies from achieving objectives they would themselves regard as being in the public interest—in this instance preventing deception of the investing public. Thus, an administrative agency may find that its own purposes are among the chief casualties of a policy of secrecy.

These are some of the compelling factors upon which the traditional American bias against secrecy in administration is based. And yet, here as elsewhere the necessity of finding a balance among competing claims remains, for executive secrecy also has its uses in a constitutional society, more so today perhaps than in the past. There is general agreement on this point with respect to national security, since there is very wide public acceptance of the need to protect military and diplomatic information from disclosure to potential national adversaries. In this area, acceptance of secrecy tends to be much too uncritical in character, and the concluding chapter of this book will attempt to demonstrate that the choice between secrecy and security is by no means as clear cut as many people imagine.

At this point, however, it is important to note that there are ways in which a certain measure of administrative privacy may contribute to the purposes as well as the survival of a constitutional society—especially the goal of protecting the individual from the arbitrary and capricious use of official power. This is so because the expansion of bureaucratic power that has occurred in recent years has placed in the hands of government officials a great deal of information on what might fairly be viewed as the private affairs of individual citizens, and the promiscuous publicizing of this information could bring serious damage to either the economic status or the personal reputation of such individuals without serving any com-

[27] *Ibid.,* p. 214.

mensurate public purpose. Insofar as rules requiring secrecy guard against this eventuality, they strengthen rather than compromise the spirit and practice of constitutionalism.

Thus the paradoxical fact is that while administrative secrecy may serve as a device for concealing an abuse of power, it is also a means by which unwarranted use of official power may itself be prevented. This is true at least as long as individuals are conceded to have a right to privacy in a democratic society—the right, that is, to be free from having their private affairs needlessly exposed to public scrutiny.[28] Not all, of course, would be prepared to acknowledge that any such right should be given serious weight in determining the proper scope of administrative secrecy. From the viewpoint of the press, for example, the transcendent character of the people's right to know makes disclosure the only policy consistent with constitutional government. And the press can find support for this identification of disclosure with constitutionalism in the fact that it is only through the intervention of the courts that executive officials have been prevented from using administrative secrecy to impair the rights of private individuals in litigation with the government. At times, however, the argument of the journalist against administrative secrecy is carried to what most people would regard as an extreme. James R. Wiggins, for example, an eloquent and persuasive spokesman for "open government" on most occasions, goes as far as to criticize the Air Force for withholding identification of accident victims until next-of-kin have been notified—on the grounds that this policy is an invasion of the people's right to know.[29]

But the fact of the matter is that there has always been a place for privacy in a free society—in such critical areas of community life as the operations of the jury room and the decision of the voter at the polling place. Cardozo's defense of

[28] For an early but perhaps still classic discussion of this right, see S. D. Warren and L. D. Brandeis, "The Right to Privacy," *Harvard Law Review*, Vol. 4 (December 1890), pp. 193–220.

[29] See *Freedom or Secrecy* (N.Y., 1956), pp. 106–108.

secrecy in jury proceedings has equal application in other areas where dispassionate deliberation is called for in the democratic process: "Freedom of debate might be stifled and independence of thought checked if jurors were made to feel that their arguments and ballots were to be freely published to the world." [30] This is not to deny that secrecy can be a dominant ideal only in an authoritarian community and that in a democratic society it can be tolerated only as an exception to the prevailing rule of publicity.

The fact that privacy has its uses could hardly be challenged by any of the critics of executive secrecy. Congressmen, for example, commonly resort to secrecy to facilitate their own deliberations. The legislative practice of convening committee meetings in executive session has long been an object of attack by the media of communication. The extent of this practice of holding closed meetings is evident from the following tabulation: [31]

Year	Total Meetings	Number Closed	Per Cent Closed
1953	2,640	892	35
1954	3,002	1,243	41
1955	2,940	1,055	36
1956	3,120	1,130	36
1957	3,251	1,103	34
1958	3,472	1,167	34
1959	3,152	940	30
1960 (Jan. 6– Mar. 31)	952	287	30

[30] As quoted in Maure L. Goldschmidt, "Publicity, Privacy and Secrecy," *The Western Political Quarterly*, Vol. 7 (September 1954), p. 405, fn. 15. A few years ago, several members of Congress became highly incensed when some enterprising social scientists attempted (with judicial consent) to eavesdrop on jury deliberations by means of a recording device as part of a general study they were conducting of jury room proceedings.

[31] See *Congressional Quarterly Weekly Report*, Vol. 17 (April 22, 1960), p. 670.

Robert Luce has given the classic defense of the secrecy which surrounds executive sessions of congressional committees:

> Behind closed doors nobody can talk to the galleries or the newspaper reporters. Buncombe is not worthwhile. Only sincerity counts. Men drop their masks. They argue to, not through, each other. That is one reason why it would be a calamity if the demand for pitiless publicity of committee deliberations should ever prevail.
>
> . . . publicity would lessen the chance for the concessions, the compromises, without which wise legislation cannot in practice be secured. Men are averse to changing their positions or yielding anything when many eyes are watching. It is in the conference room that agreements are reached, results accomplished.[32]

Newspapermen themselves have been quick to claim the privilege of privacy in refusing to divulge the identity of confidential informants to the press—a refusal that has on occasion gotten them into trouble with the law.[33] Nor has the scientific community itself been averse to using secrecy when it has served its purposes. The views of one distinguished scientific critic of executive secrecy, Dr. Arthur H. Compton, have been described as follows:

> As he talked, it became apparent that he was an enemy of governmental secrecy chiefly because he felt that it inconvenienced scientists and science. Where he felt it might work to the advantage of science or any other institution of which he approved, he had no objections.[34]

The truth of the matter is that there is no major institution or profession in American life that does not find some measure of privacy useful for the achievement of its special objectives.

---

[32] *Congress: An Explanation* (Cambridge, Mass., 1926), pp. 12–13.

[33] See, for example, the recent case involving a *New York Herald Tribune* reporter, *Garland* v. *Torre*, 259 F. 2d. 545 (1958).

[34] Richard Rovere, "Letter from Washington," *The New Yorker*, (May 16, 1959), p. 96.

Of course executive officials have themselves contributed a great deal to their own difficulties by following a policy of duplicity where administrative secrecy is concerned. One of the worst examples of this is the practice of leaking a one-sided version of events from executive files that are otherwise closed to the public. This partial disclosure of information may permit the executive to shape public opinion in ways that would not be possible if the whole story were made immediately available for critical appraisal. And, as the Dixon-Yates and other episodes suggest, administrative secrecy may be used for no higher purpose than to conceal dubious conduct on the part of executive officials. The case for legitimate privacy in governmental affairs is constantly being compromised by unwarranted secrecy.

The Politics of Secrecy

Reconciling the conflicting interests that converge upon administrative secrecy presents a complex task for public policy. By and large, the judiciary would appear to have gone far toward the solution of at least one major problem—the protection of private rights against the worst effects of executive secrecy in proceedings before the courts. The rules that have been developed through judicial decision up to this point strike a reasonable balance among the disparate public and private interests affected by the practice of secrecy in litigation. The one notable exception would appear to be the decision of the Supreme Court in *Reynolds* v. *United States*, where the high court departed from the very reasonable formula of compromise that had been worked out in related though not identical cases. This was the principle that the government is entitled to keep its secrets when it deems this necessary, but that the cause of justice to private litigants is best served if it is

obliged simultaneously to forfeit its case in court if these
secrets are relevant to deciding the matter on hand.

But while the judiciary can do much to provide a remedy
against the abuse of private rights, it can do little to keep open
the channels of information through which the public is kept
broadly informed of the affairs of state. The "openness" of
government is largely dependent upon the outcome of the
perennial institutional conflict between the president and Congress over administrative secrecy, a conflict in which the president as a rule is ranged on the side of secrecy and the legislature
on the side of disclosure, at least as far as executive activities
are concerned. It is also affected by the continuing efforts of
the media of communication to push back the frontiers of secrecy presently defended by bureaucracy. As long as Congress
and these media exhibit resourcefulness in penetrating and exposing the affairs of bureaucracy, American administration is
as likely to be characterized by extravagant publicity as it is
by excessive secrecy.

During recent years this resourcefulness has been very much
in evidence. In the period immediately following World War
II, the need for secrecy received extensive support, in both a
formal way through statutes, executive orders, and presidential directives, and informally through the great variety of
psychological inducements to secrecy that have developed
around the operations of the classification system in defense
agencies. At the same time, however, criticism of excessive secrecy has also found firm institutional expression, most dra-
matically through the work of the House Subcommittee on
Government Information and the companion activities of the
Senate Subcommittee on Constitutional Rights.

The Moss subcommittee alone numbers several achievements
to its credit. Thus far its investigations have led not only, as
previously discussed, to a revision of the basic statute governing administrative housekeeping, so as to reduce the likeli-

hood of this law being used to support unnecessary secrecy, but also to the elimination of many administrative regulations and procedures which had encouraged executive agencies to withhold information needlessly. The Department of Defense established an Office of Declassification Policy in an effort to cut down on the backlog of classified material stored in government warehouses, and in July, 1960, it instituted the system of automatic declassification of documents over a twelve-year period. The Department of Agriculture developed arrangements for releasing information concerning the activities of its advisory committees. And a variety of other agencies, including the Bureau of Customs, the General Services Administration, and the Federal National Mortgage Association, have revised their information practices to permit greater disclosure of official information to the public. As one witness before the subcommittee noted:

> This subcommittee has already done a great deal to expedite the flow of Government information. The mere fact that this committee was created, that it has raised questions, that it has solicited information from Government agencies on information policies—all have helped to improve current information practices.[35]

Simultaneously, groups such as the American Society of Newspaper Editors and Sigma Delta Chi, the honorary journalism fraternity, working particularly through their freedom of information committees, have kept up unrelenting pressure for more permissive policies in the field of government information. Many of the hearings of the Moss subcommittee have been held as a result of complaints from reporters that they were denied access to official data by government agencies, and the work of the committee has received frequent in-

[35] *Twenty-Fifth Intermediate Report of the Committee on Government Operations,* 84th Cong., 2d sess., House Report No. 2947, July 27, 1956, p. 78.

dorsement in newspaper editorials and at meetings of press associations across the country. The extent and character of the collaboration that has developed between the Moss subcommittee and the newspaper community is suggested by the following case:

> The *Portland Journal* in Portland, Oregon, requested access to a Veterans Administration report on residential lot values in the Portland metropolitan area. The report was prepared for the Veterans Administration by a group of non-Government real estate appraisers. After VA officials refused to make the report public, the *Portland Journal* contacted Herbert Brucker, chairman of the freedom of information committee of the American Society of Newspaper Editors. Mr. Brucker complained to the Special Subcommittee on Government Information that refusal of the report restricted access to public information.
>
> The Committee Report on Survey and Residential Lot Value Opinions, dated July 25, 1956, was made public by the Veterans Administration after the agency was contacted by the subcommittee.[36]

Aside from the question of whether the committee's success in forcing the disclosure of information has always been in the public interest, its record thus far gives ample assurance that —apart perhaps from the affairs of military agencies—administrative officials are quite defensive about withholding information and are reluctant to persist in practices of secrecy when these practices are exposed to public view or come under congressional criticism. This reluctance springs in some measure from the fact that the political beliefs of administrators have been framed in the same ideological tradition as those of

[36] *Second Report by the Committee on Government Operations,* 85th Cong., 1st sess., House Report No. 157, Feb. 22, 1957, p. 43. According to a tabulation prepared by the committee, approximately one-third of the investigations it has conducted of administrative secrecy have been prompted by complaints from newspapermen. See *Twenty-Fourth Report by the Committee on Government Operations,* 86th Cong., 2d sess., House report no. 2084, July 2, 1960, pp. 4–35.

Congressmen and newspaper editors. But whether the ideological commitment on the part of executive officials to freedom of information be strong or weak, this does not disparage the role that congressional and public scrutiny play in prodding the administrator's conscience, for it cannot be denied that the tradition of disclosure might wither in the shade of administrative evasion or inertia were it not for the continued exercise of outside vigilance.

PART TWO

THE POWER OF PUBLICITY

CHAPTER 6

GOVERNMENT REGULATION
THROUGH PUBLICITY

DISCUSSIONS of social control in civilized societies generally turn on the assumption that the principal penalties that government officials can direct against lawbreaking are the ordinary fines and imprisonments provided for in a legal code. The governmental role in the total process of law enforcement has thus been pictured as restricted mainly to the application of formal sanctions. As a matter of fact, the historical origins of government have been traced to the need for institutionalizing explicit methods of restraint when, at rather obscure breaking-points in social development, control through informal mechanisms such as custom and public opinion no longer remained feasible. This can occur when a society moves from simple to more complex patterns of social organization or when it seeks to meet the threat of disorganization inherent in rapid social change.[1]

Consequently, heavy reliance upon such an informal punishment as adverse public opinion to prevent and punish viola-

---

[1] See, for example, John Dickinson, "Social Order and Political Authority," *American Political Science Review*, Vol. 23 (May, August, 1929), pp. 293–328, 593–632, especially pp. 305–308; E. Adamson Hoebel, *The Law of Primitive Man* (Cambridge, 1954), pp. 293–94, 330.

tions of community law has hitherto been regarded as a distinctive mark of relatively primitive social systems—societies without government or with only embryonic governmental forms. The effectiveness of the publicity sanction in this kind of simple community stems in good part from the frequency of interaction and communication among members of the group, conditions which quicken and intensify the punitive weight of public disfavor. This disfavor may manifest itself actively by ridicule or passively by the withdrawal of association. The intimacy of association characteristic of tribal communities was an early casualty of social evolution, and as individual relationships have acquired an anonymous character, it is ordinarily assumed that publicity has lost much of its importance as a method of control.

However, in view of the fact that the publicity sanction depends for its effectiveness upon the ease of communications within a community,[2] it follows that as what is commonly called mass society has moved toward greater interaction among its members, through, for example, developments and improvements in communications technology, it has paved the way for a revival in the influence that public opinion can exert over personal conduct. And the testimony of Riesman and others would suggest that, as a result of this and other factors, individual behavior has in recent times come under just such increasing direction and control from public opinion, especially in modern American society.[3]

One of the most important aspects of this development is the extension of the use of publicity into a method of coercion in the hands of government officials. Here we are referring

[2] For rather striking evidence of the existence of such a relationship, see Richard D. Schwartz, "Social Factors in the Development of Legal Control: A Case Study of Two Israeli Settlements," *Yale Law Journal*, Vol. 63 (February, 1954), pp. 471–91.

[3] This is of course the principal thesis of *The Lonely Crowd* (New Haven, 1950).

not to the spontaneous subjection of the individual to cues and directions he receives from the public of which he is a member,[4] but rather to governmental use or threat to use the sanction of adverse publicity as a means of controlling the behavior of individuals under its jurisdiction. In this instance the state does not apply, it only initiates the application of a punishment. The penalties attached to adverse publicity are actually imposed by the public itself. But the increasing ability of government to instigate the application of these penalties has brought about a significant extension in its control capacity. A technique of restraint once thought exclusively suitable for use in small societies without government has in fact become one of the most formidable methods of coercion available, in complex modern societies, to the state itself. At the same time, however, an important source of disequilibrium has been introduced in the precarious balance between individual autonomy and social control through which democratic government attempts to secure justice.

It should be noted that this use of the publicity sanction is not the only method by which government officials have today acquired the power to inflict damage upon private individuals without necessary resort to formal prosecution, or in constitutional language, "due process of law." Similar in its informal coercive effect to the publicity sanction is the ability of government to deny or withdraw access to the expanding list of privileges it has come to control, including government employment, educational scholarships, access to public housing, passports, and a variety of similar benefits.[5] It was at one time thought possible to curb abuse in the exercise

[4] An analysis of the role of this type of control in organized society may be found in Robert A. Dahl and Charles E. Lindblom, *Politics, Economics and Welfare* (New York, 1953), pp. 99–104.

[5] See Note, "Judicial Acquiescence in the Forfeiture of Constitutional Rights through Expansion of the Conditioned Privilege Doctrine," *Indiana Law Journal*, Vol. 28 (Summer, 1953), pp. 520–44.

of discretionary power in the hands of executive agencies by making the administrative process more judicial in character. This was a chief purpose of the Administrative Procedure Act of 1946. But, as one observer pointed out, the terms even of this act leave completely unguarded a "huge portion of administrative discretionary power which lies beyond the reach of both judicial review and procedural safeguards." [6] The ability of government agencies to exert informal pressure is not entirely curbed by restrictions upon their capacity to inflict punishment through regular legal channels.

The coming power and scope of publicity as an instrument of law enforcement in modern society was forecast at the beginning of this century by Edward A. Ross in a pioneer study of social control:

> Signs are not wanting that in the future an increasing restraint will be exercised through public opinion, and that this kind of control will gain at the expense of other kinds. For one thing, this form of coercion is suited to the type of man created by modern life. Only the criminal or moral hero cares not how others may think of him. The growing rage for publicity and the craving for notoriety shows that the men of to-day respond warmly to praise and wilt quickly under general disapproval. Then, too, certain social developments favor the ascendancy of the public. The growing economic interdependence and the closer interweaving of private interests mean that the individual gives hostages to the community for his good behavior. . . . The more frequent contacts of men and the better facilities for forming and focusing the opinion of the public tend in the same direction. . . .
>
> With a democratic, forward-looking people like ours, opinion, no longer split up into small currents by class lines or broken in force by masses of family, sect, or caste tradition, the

[6] Kenneth C. Davis, *Administrative Law* (St. Paul, 1951), p. 137. Chap. 4 contains a comprehensive discussion of aspects of administrative regulatory power that lie beyond the reach of legislative and judicial limitations upon the abuse of executive authority.

debris of the past, acquires a tidal volume and sweep. In such a stream all oaks become reeds. The day of the sturdy backwoodsman, settler, flat-boatman, or prospector, defiant not only of law but of public opinion as well, is gone never to return.[7]

What Ross did not envisage when he wrote these lines was the development of publicity as an instrument of government control, since, like most sociologists, he tended to juxtapose social control through public opinion with government control by law. In point of fact, as this chapter will attempt to show, publicity as well as law can become a pervasive instrument of regulation by governmental agencies.

Congressional Use of Publicity

Publicity has long had a variety of uses for Congress as for all legislative bodies. Of no small importance is the fact that such publicity provides an avenue whereby the legislature can vie with the executive in a quest for the attention of the community, in much the same way as it competes for the other means and ends of power that are at stake in conflict between the two branches of government. As long ago as 1908, Woodrow Wilson traced the president's supremacy over Congress to his ability to focus public attention upon himself,[8] and the executive advantage in this regard has been more than reinforced by developments since that time in the technology of mass communications. The presidential ascendancy characteristic of twentieth-century American politics is frequently traced to the privileged access of the president to radio, television, and the news columns of the press.[9]

[7] Edward A. Ross, *Social Control* (New York, 1901), pp. 104–105.
[8] *Constitutional Government in the United States* (New York, 1908), pp. 67–69.
[9] See in this regard Sidney Hyman, *The American President* (New York, 1954), pp. 101–104. One of the principal avenues of presidential influence in

From this point of view the recent upsurge in congressional investigations primarily reflects an attempt on the part of the legislature to restore a balance of power in the area of publicity. No aspect of congressional activity other than investigations is as capable of attracting the attention of the public and of the communications facilities that both direct and reflect public interest. Investigations are a form of entertainment, even if they stir in the minds of some observers recollections of the Roman amphitheater or of the public trials and executions of revolutionary regimes.[10] But since investigations have such dramatic value—even reminiscent in their effect of Aristotle's venerable description of tragedy in his *Poetics:* "through pity and fear effecting a proper purgation of these emotions"— they can compete with the other forms of entertainment with which politics and political events are in competition for the voter's attention.[11] Otherwise, Congress might be entirely up-staged before the national audience by the presidential office and the activities of its incumbent. In short, the preoccupation of Congress with its investigative role may be said to spring from the very realistic legislative perception that a president cutting a cake has more news value for the media of communication than almost anything a congressman does in his non-investigative capacities.

As a method of redressing the balance of power with the executive with respect to command of public attention, the publicity connected with investigations may be said to serve

the field of publicity is the press conference. For a recent treatment of this subject see Elmer E. Cornwell, Jr., "The Presidential Press Conference: A Study in Institutionalization," *Midwest Journal of Political Science,* Vol. IV (November 1960), pp. 370–89.

[10] Recent critical discussions of congressional investigations include Alan Barth, *Government by Investigation* (New York, 1955); and Telford Taylor, *Grand Inquest: The Story of Congressional Investigations* (New York, 1955).

[11] See the discussion of "politics as an object of consumption" in Riesman, *op. cit.,* pp. 212–14. See also Morris Rosenberg, "The Meaning of Politics in Mass Society," *Public Opinion Quarterly,* Vol. 15 (Spring, 1951), pp. 14–15.

a function for Congress as an institution. An additional legislative purpose furthered by such publicity has long been recognized in the literature on investigations. This is the function of attracting public support for pending or proposed laws, or publicizing the existence of abuses that may need congressional action.[12] Taking, apparently, as a point of departure the assumption that investigations should always be directed at the enactment or modification of law, severe criticism has sometimes been directed at congressional inquiries that do not culminate in statutory proposals. This criticism tends, whatever its other merits, to ignore the other functions of investigations, including the extent to which publicity in itself may be a corrective, eliminating in some instances the need for legislation by bringing about a process of self-regulation by the group under scrutiny.

Its value from an institutional point of view may thus be said to have made at least some contribution to the favorable attitude taken by congressmen toward the publicity connected with legislative investigations. It goes without saying, of course, that the publicity attached to investigations may also serve a wide variety of self-interested purposes for congressmen or congressional blocs. The fact that prominence in a well-publicized investigation has enormous self-promotional possibilities for the individual legislator needs no documentation here. As the examples of Kefauver and Nixon in recent history reveal, the power of publicity can easily short-circuit the traditional dependence of the individual legislator upon length of service for power and prestige. An index of legislative recognition of this fact is provided by the increasing tendency of congressmen to relate their preferences for committee assignments to the publicity surrounding the work of

[12] Martin N. McGeary, *The Developments of Congressional Investigative Power* (New York, 1940), gives considerable attention to this function of the investigative process.

the committees concerned.[13] This may be a more important factor in congressional choice among committee seats today than the traditional interest of the legislator in placing himself upon committees related in their jurisdiction to the particular economic and social interests of his constituency.

Parenthetically, it should be noted that congressmen are not the only public officials aware of the self-serving implications of the publicity connected with their role. Judges, for example, are by no means immune to the temptation to exploit official power for personal publicity. One writer has commented that "Publicity-loving showoffs on the bench have become such a menace that in many courts, such as one I visited in Missouri, smart defense attorneys plead with reporters to leave the room during the hearing of their cases 'so the judge won't throw the book at the prisoner to get his name in the papers.' A Cincinnati judge justified this practice with the explanation: 'It's just like any other selling job. If people keep seeing your name in the paper, they recognize it on the ballot.' "[14] And as subsequent discussion will show, executive officials are prey to the same temptations.

For congressional blocs, whether organized on party or factional lines, the publicity evoking characteristic of investigations is of considerable practical utility, providing, as it does, the opportunity of inflicting public embarrassment upon executive agencies, or, if the legislative inclination so directs, private institutions or individuals. The manipulation of such publicity has become a strategic factor in party as well as factional warfare in our political system. From the point of view of some investigators, the most advantageous aspect of this

[13] It was reported in 1951 that no less than one hundred representatives were seeking seats on the House Un-American Activities Committee. See Irving Dilliard, "Congressional Investigations: the Role of the Press," *University of Chicago Law Review*, Vol. 18 (Spring, 1951), pp. 585-90, at p. 590.

[14] Morton Sontheimer, "Our Reeking Halls of Justice," *Collier's*, Vol. 123, No. 14, at pp. 19, 77 (April 2, 1949).

publicity is the fact that their own investment before the public eye is merely one of legitimate legislative curiosity, while the group under scrutiny is necessarily put upon the defensive, a posture from which full recovery before the bar of public opinion is often very difficult to attain.

The power of publicity has found its most graphic illustration in contemporary legislative politics through the career of Senator Joseph McCarthy. The web of McCarthy's influence was woven almost entirely out of the fabric of publicity. It rested in part on the fact that there was a wide and deep public support for a vigorous anti-communist policy, however carried out, and McCarthy was able to identify himself as one of communism's most stalwart foes. And in part also, it stemmed from the intimidation of McCarthy's fellow politicians, as well as leaders in other walks of life, who were fearful lest a collision with McCarthy bring them the reputation of being sympathetic toward communism. But if publicity was the source of McCarthy's strength, it also proved ultimately to be his undoing. For in the Army-McCarthy hearings, where he and his staff were exposed in a baleful light, he suddenly found himself with a firm grip on the wrong end of the publicity stick, and it proved a disaster from which he never recovered.

Publicity has traditionally been used with great effectiveness by Congress to throw light upon the misdeeds of executive officials. More recently, it has acquired increasing prominence in connection with legislative investigations aimed at ferreting out wrongdoing in various areas of private life. It is this present-day preoccupation of many legislative committees with illegal or unethical activity within society that has transformed some legislative hearings into legislative courts and led to mounting pressure for reform of investigative procedures. Such pressure is quite similar to that generated more than a decade ago in favor of reforming the administrative process, when it appeared that executive agencies were over-reaching their proper authority.[15]

While acting as auxiliary and *ad hoc* instruments of law enforcement, legislative committees have no power to impose punitive legal sanctions, except indirectly for a refusal to answer questions. Nevertheless, their direct power to punish is considerable. The core of this power is the ability of a committee to inflict the penalty of adverse publicity upon those called before it. This sanction has been used with telling effect in such widely diverse areas as the investigation of subversive activity, gambling, and the rigging of television quiz programs.

In calling witnesses to public hearings for the purpose, for example, of exposing what is considered to be either illegal or immoral activity, a legislative committee has the visible and usually justified expectation that such exposure will at the very least bring unfavorable public attention to the individuals concerned. Aside from the psychic deprivation or loss of public esteem that this exposure may represent for the person involved, such other extra-legal sanctions may follow in the wake of an appearance at a public hearing as loss of employment. Publicity may thus operate as a sanction in and of itself, or it may initiate the application of other informal penalties. The total impact of the sanction applied may bear some resemblance to the ostracism sometimes imposed by primitive societies.[16]

Not the least impressive illustration of the force of the pub-

[15] An interesting illustration of the correlation between a group's opinion and its interest is provided by the fact that the liberal-conservative alignment on the question of reforming the law enforcement procedures of Congress is exactly the opposite from what it was in the struggle over reform of the administrative process. In the case of administration, Senator McCarran, for example, whose position may reasonably be described as conservative, was a sponsor of reform; in the case of Congress he was a target of reformers.

[16] See in this regard the discussion of "outlawry" in Taylor, *op. cit.*, Appendix III.

licity sanction in recent days may be found in the unhappy fate of Charles Van Doren, dismissed from his position on the Columbia University faculty, as well as his post as a consultant to the National Broadcasting Company, after his exposure before a congressional investigating committee as a participant in the practice of "rigging" television quiz shows. However, an even more poignant indication of the cutting edge of publicity as a method of punishment is the fact that some individuals have committed suicide in recent years as a result of their involvement in legislative inquiries, including E. H. Norman, a Canadian government official, and William K. Sherwood, a California scientist. In each case the suicide was connected with the fact that the individual in question had been linked through congressional publicity with Communist or subversive activities.

Legislative use of the publicity sanction as a method of control is not confined to its employment in the investigative process. Some statutes passed by the legislature also depend for their enforcement upon the effectiveness of publicity in preventing undesirable conduct. This is true of lobbying legislation, for example. The premise upon which the Federal Regulation of Lobbying Act of 1946 rests is that the mere publication of information about the activities of lobbyists will itself, given the disrepute in which such activities are presumed to be held by the public, help to keep lobbying within bounds. The same expectation is visible in the Internal Security Act of 1950, which requires Communist front groups to so identify themselves in their published material. There would appear to be little doubt that identification as a Communist organization would dissipate whatever persuasive effectiveness a political group might otherwise have upon the American public. It is, however, also clear that other legislation dependent for its effectiveness upon the publicity sanction may be toothless or bite very deeply, depending in good part upon the intensity of public disapproval of the activity against which the legislation is directed. It is still an open question as to whether recent efforts to regulate the internal affairs of trade unions through disclosure statutes will prove effective, given the fact that labor organizations like the Teamsters Union have, through long years of adversity, become accustomed to operating in an atmosphere of unfavorable public attention.

Administrative Regulation through Publicity

The visibility of administrative as distinguished from legislative use of publicity as a method of regulation is comparatively dim. This is true in some degree because a large part of administrative resort to publicity as a coercive device has been concentrated in areas of social and economic regulation without the attention-claiming characteristic of, for example, congressional investigations into vice and subversion. More important, however, it is a product of the fact that administrative use of publicity in law enforcement has concentrated upon the threat of adverse publicity in a pre-trial proceeding, itself unpublicized, rather than the actual application of the sanction in formal hearings. In such instances, it is even to the advantage of those intimidated by the threat of adverse publicity to conceal the fact that any such coercion has occurred.

The use of publicity as an enforcement technique by administrative agencies has aroused comparatively little concern in Congress. Witness the fact, previously noted, that Congress included no provision restricting the use of publicity as a coercive device in the Administrative Procedure Act of 1946. This congressional indifference to the possibility of administrative misuse of the power of publicity ignored the evidence contained in such earlier studies of the regulatory process as that undertaken by the attorney-general's Committee on

Administrative Procedure. The report of this committee was the most important link in the chain of events out of which legislation designed to reform administrative procedures emerged, and in its discussion of the enforcement activities of the Federal Alcohol Administration, the committee had plainly stated the problem of publicity: "So marked has the fear of disastrous publicity become that many permittees have settled cases by sacrificing *bona fide* defenses, in order to avoid the issuance of a press release. In some instances, the Committee has reluctantly concluded, the former Federal Alcohol Administration appears to have relied upon threatened adverse publicity as an extra-legal sanction to secure observance of its commands, even when the validity of its dictates was not free from doubt." [17]

The problem to which the committee was here calling attention was the authority vested in national regulatory agencies to issue a press release at the time judicial action was first initiated against persons suspected of violating the law. This press release, detailing the character of a suspected offense and the culprit involved, inflicted immediate damage upon the reputation of a defendant even before a formal finding of guilt or innocence had been made. In its final report, the committee majority side-stepped the problem of controlling this use of publicity with the suggestion that the matter be made subject to further study.[18] However, a minority report submitted by three members of the committee gave special attention to what it called the "vexatious subject" of administrative use of publicity in enforcement proceedings and recommended that "in all contested proceedings, agency publicity shall be withheld during preliminary or investigative phases of adjudication." [19]

[17] United States Attorney-General's Committee on Administrative Procedure, *Administrative Procedure in Government Agencies* (Washington, 1941), pp. 134–35.
[18] *Ibid.*, p. 194.
[19] *Ibid.*, p. 221.

It was because of the publicity attendant upon its use that Landis called the power to prosecute the most dangerous area of discretion open to administrative officials.[20] This conviction is echoed in a more recent discussion of the prosecuting power, where it is pointed out that "proof of innocence seldom removes the scars of public accusation and public trial." [21] At its worst the power to prosecute may afford the opportunity to impose the publicity sanction in the absence of any intention or capacity to bring a defendant to trial. One of the criticisms levelled against OPA enforcement during World War II was that in some instances charges were filed against business concerns when there was no prospect that OPA officials would allow these publicized allegations to be tested in court. Instead, it was alleged, the intention of the price control agency was merely that of calling public attention to its enforcement program. Suspicion that this was the case led some newspapers to initiate a policy of non-publication of OPA releases on impending proceedings.[22]

The task of preventing any improper use of the publicity sanction prior to a formal determination of the guilt of a defendant is complicated by the fact that in some areas such publicity serves a useful if not indispensable control function. In, for example, the enforcement of legislation protecting the consumer against the manufacture and sale of impure food and drugs, the capacity of administrative agencies to inform the public that a product is suspected of containing harmful ingredients may play an invaluable role in preventing its consumption until the accuracy of this administrative suspicion can be determined. It was with this consideration in mind that

[20] James Landis, *The Administrative Process* (New Haven, 1938), pp. 110–11.

[21] Davis, *op. cit.*, p. 161. See also Note, "Prosecutor's Discretion," *University of Pennsylvania Law Review*, Vol. 103 (June, 1955), pp. 1057–87.

[22] For a discussion of this practice see Marshall B. Clinard, *The Black Market* (New York, 1952), pp. 86–87.

the Food and Drug Administration was authorized by statute to issue press releases warning the public against the use of products suspected of involving "imminent danger to health or gross deception to consumers."

The scope of this kind of power was given dramatic illustration on November 9, 1959, when the Secretary of Health, Education, and Welfare Arthur S. Flemming, acting on the basis of information he received from the Food and Drug Administration, issued a statement to the press in which he noted that cranberries grown in Washington and Oregon showed contamination from aminotriazole, a weed-killer that experiments had shown capable of producing cancerous growth in the thyroid of rats. Flemming advised housewives not to purchase cranberries until it could be ascertained whether or not the berries they were buying were actually free from contamination.

Coming as it did just prior to the Thanksgiving and Christmas holiday season, this announcement could not have been more disadvantageously timed from the point of view of the cranberry industry. As the impact of Flemming's warning was felt across the country, cancellation orders came pouring into Ocean Spray Cranberries, Inc., a co-operative which marketed 75 per cent of the nation's cranberry crop. Restaurants took cranberries off the menu, and stores removed the product from their shelves. State health officials in Ohio, along with city authorities in Chicago and San Francisco, banned the sale of all cranberries within their jurisdiction.

Needless to say, the cranberry growers themselves were highly incensed by Flemming's announcement and its economic consequences. Growers freely predicted that his action would have a disastrous effect upon the marketing of their crops, and the Ocean Spray association announced that it would seek reimbursement of $100,000,000 from the federal government. Statements sympathizing with the plight of the industry came from many quarters, and it became almost *de rigeur* for candidates engaged in preliminary jockeying for the 1960 presidential nominations to eat cranberries in public with good humor if not with gusto. (Eventually the cranberry industry suffered damages estimated to run as high as $40,000,000. Secretary of Agriculture Benson later announced that about $10,000,000 would be paid by the government as an indemnity to the industry.)

Another vivid illustration of the utility of publicity in administrative regulation was the action of the Public Health Service in giving immediate national publicity to its withdrawal of approval from the polio vaccine manufactured by the Cutter Laboratories in California, after several children inoculated with the vaccine came down with polio in 1955. Upon hearing this announcement, several localities immediately held up their inoculation programs, until it could be ascertained whether the vaccine they were using came from the Cutter firm. Several months later the Public Health Service was to acknowledge that a failure in its own safety tests had been principally responsible for the fact that live virus was contained in the Cutter vaccine. But Cutter Laboratories ultimately suffered a loss of $1,209,000 in 1955, as compared with earnings of $676,037 in 1954. In this case as in others, both the social utility of the publicity sanction, and its punitive effect, possibly unwarranted, were made simultaneously clear.

The persistent strain between the public and private interest in the use of the publicity sanction is also pointed up in the area of penal administration. The publication of the names of individuals paroled from prison can clearly be justified as a means of alerting the public to the presence of possibly unreformed criminals in the community and of preventing abuse of the parole power by state governors. However, it can with equal vigor be condemned as a serious impediment to the re-

habilitation of ex-convicts, insofar as it strips away the anonymity upon which public acceptance of these individuals
may depend. And in the field of welfare administration, there
is still serious disagreement between those who argue for the
publication of the names of persons receiving old-age assistance
payments, as a means of deterring fraudulent claims, and
those who contend that even the poverty stricken have a right
to privacy.

Whether or not it is applied beforehand, the penalty of
adverse publicity has an obvious impact as part of the total
punishment imposed on individuals found guilty of violating
all statutes enforced by regulatory agencies. Indeed this unfavorable publicity may be the most important part of the
punishment received on such occasions. This factor needs to
be taken into account in any assessment of the total weight
of sanction attached to violations of regulatory legislation.[23]
These laws are frequently criticized on the grounds that the
formal penalties they provide for violations are too trivial to
deter potential offenders. This criticism, however reasonable
on its face, tends to overlook entirely the deterrent effect of
fear of adverse publicity. Certainly, in contemplating behavior
likely to be held in violation of a regulatory statute, a business
firm risks, in the possible loss of public esteem, a highly vital
economic asset—beside which the possibility of a minor fine
may pale in significance.

The potential value of publicity as a deterrent in law enforcement may be especially noticeable in its absence. A number of studies of juvenile delinquency have argued that the
immunity granted juvenile offenders from publicity at the
time of their arrest is a key factor in the growth of delinquency. As one report put it: "Many parents have greater fear

[23] See the discussion of this problem in Emmette S. Redford, *Administration of National Economic Control* (New York, 1952), pp. 169–74.

of their neighbors learning of their children's misdeeds than they do of the penalty the law may inflict." [24] This argument may or may not be valid, and it certainly ignores the very positive values served by privacy in juvenile proceedings. But it is by no means implausible that law enforcement *per se* would be weakened by the absence of publicity in connection with juvenile offenses.

Informal Adjudication

Perhaps the best evidence of the power of publicity may be found in the success achieved by regulatory agencies in using the mere threat of adverse public attention to bring about the settlement of complaints without the necessity of formal hearings. Obviously, fear of adverse publicity is not the sole factor involved in the successful employment by regulatory agencies of this informal adjudication—a process that has become so commonplace that it is now called the "lifeblood of the administrative process." [25] The willingness of defendants to admit or compromise their disagreements with complaints lodged against them by regulatory agencies is also the product of such factors as the desire to avoid the expense and uncertainty of formal litigation and an ambition to cultivate the good will of government officials. Nevertheless, the threat of adverse publicity resulting from appearance at a formal hearing before a regulatory tribunal is a central factor in the total process of extra-legal coercion involved in informal adjudication.

Much has been made, for example, of the value of threatened publicity in effecting the conspicuously successful rec-

---

[24] *New York Times*, March 27, 1955, p. 55.

[25] The phrase is from the United States Attorney-General's Committee on Administrative Procedure, *op. cit.*, p. 35. It is used as the point of departure for the very thorough discussion of informal adjudication to be found in Walter Gellhorn, *Federal Administrative Proceedings* (Baltimore, 1941), Chap. 2.

ord of the Securities and Exchange Commission in controlling
the investment field without the necessity of formal litigation.[26]
Only rarely has the SEC found it necessary to hold a public
hearing in connection with its regulation of the marketing of
securities. Fear of the adverse publicity connected with the
public airing of a complaint has been a sufficient pressure to
bring about compliance with SEC suggestions for alterations
in the language of a prospectus. This is so, of course, largely because successful flotation of an issue of stock demands absolute confidence in the integrity of the product offered for
purchase by investors. Any publicity as to the existence of
doubt regarding the truth of claims made in a prospectus would
almost certainly have a fatal effect upon the sale of the securities concerned.

Other national regulatory agencies have likewise used the
threat of unfavorable publicity to buttress their regulatory
power, especially in the field of banking. However, one national agency, the Federal Trade Commission, has followed
the practice of requiring firms that have waived their right to
a public hearing to file stipulations making public acknowledgement of the truth of allegations contained in a complaint.[27]
This policy reduces the ability of the commission to use the
threat of unfavorable publicity to force the informal settlement of complaints, since the defendant has to make clear
public acknowledgement of guilt even when he agrees not to
dispute the charges lodged against him. Consequently, adherence to this procedure could be cited as among the factors

[26] Discussions of the SEC's reliance upon the fear of publicity in its enforcement activities may be found in Davis, *op. cit.*, pp. 150–52; Landis,
op. cit., pp. 108–10; and Joseph P. Chamberlain, Noel T. Dowling and Paul R.
Hays, *The Judicial Function in Federal Administrative Agencies* (New York,
1942), pp. 115–18. Chap. 3 of this last named work contains the best discussion of the use of the publicity sanction in law enforcement to be found in the
literature on administrative regulation.

[27] See Kenneth C. Davis, *Administrative Law Treatise* (St. Paul, 1958),
Vol. I, pp. 237–40.

that have handicapped the success of the FTC's enforcement program in the past. It is, however, a moot point as to whether public support of fair competition is sufficient to make the publicity sanction of compelling importance in the regulation of competitive practices among business firms today.

One of the most famous of all attempts to use the publicity sanction in national administrative regulation came with the establishment of the National Recovery Administration in 1934. The NRA relied almost entirely upon its blue eagle symbol as a means of imposing codes of fair competition upon broad segments of American industry. It withheld the right to display this emblem from firms which refused to co-operate in renouncing the practices of cut-throat competition which NRA officials regarded as being primarily responsible for demoralizing the economy. For a time at least, the NRA succeeded in making the blue eagle a virtual symbol of national patriotism.

> The new emblem became the focus of moral and civic pressure. Parades celebrated it. Speeches praised it. Throughout the land merchants put the Blue Eagle in their windows and stamped it on their products. Over two million employers signed up. Consumers signed a pledge of their own. . . .
>
> The climax came with the Blue Eagle parade in New York City early in September. In the greatest march in the city's history, a quarter of a million men and women streamed down Fifth Avenue, while a million and a half more lined the streets, watching and cheering. . . . On it went till midnight in a pandemonium of ticker tape, enthusiasm, and fellowship. The flight of the Blue Eagle had reached its zenith.[28]

In state regulation also, the threat of adverse publicity has come to play an important role in the informal enforcement

[28] Arthur M. Schlesinger, Jr., *The Coming of the New Deal* (Boston, 1959), pp. 115–16.

of administrative law. One of the areas of state administration in which its effectiveness has been most recently proved is in the operation of newly enacted state fair-employment practice acts. In this case the effectiveness of the publicity sanction has been vital to the success of the legislation concerned, since the assumption upon which FEP laws were enacted was that the law could be administered with a minimum of resort to formal litigation.[29] This conciliation philosophy, which has been at the core of all FEP enforcement programs, is rooted in the consideration that excessive reliance upon legal coercion would be in ill accord with a basic purpose of fair employment legislation—the improvement of group relations. The image of constraint associated with frequent resort to enforcement through courtroom proceedings could very well alienate the public from both an FEP agency and the groups whose welfare it seeks to advance. Even if this were not the case, a factor impelling avoidance of litigation by FEP agencies is the practical difficulty of proving discrimination or intent to discriminate through evidence that will stand up in court.

Thus, if it were necessary to rely upon formal legal sanctions for enforcement purposes, it is doubtful if FEP laws would be capable of effective enforcement at all. The fact that fair employment agencies have by and large written a successful enforcement record is, therefore, impressive testimony to their ability to dispose of complaints without formal process. From its establishment in 1945 through 1951 the New York agency found it necessary to hold a formal hearing in connection with only one of the 507 validated complaints lodged with it.[30] Of course in many of these cases coercion against

---

[29] See *State and Municipal Fair Employment Legislation,* United States Senate, Committee on Labor and Public Welfare, 82d Cong., 2d sess. (Washington, 1953), p. 12.

[30] Louis Ruchames, *Race, Jobs and Politics* (New York, 1953), p. 169. During a more recent year, 1959, the New York agency reported that it had

the person named in a complaint as guilty of discrimination was unnecessary, since the act to which the complaint referred sprang from ignorance either of the law or of the fact that the particular act was prohibited by it. But where constraint has been needed, one of the most important factors working in behalf of FEP agencies has been an unwillingness on the part of those against whom discrimination has been alleged to have the charges against them publicized at a formal hearing. In the states in which it has been possible to enact FEP laws, the publicity connected with such a hearing is in itself punishment, whatever the verdict of a hearing tribunal may be. From the point of view of a business firm it becomes a vital necessity to avoid such a hearing, since public relations considerations must be given precedence over whatever estimate the firm may make of its legal position in a case. As one study of fair employment administration concluded: "embarrassment not harassment or punishment is the chief sanction." [31]

The fact that adverse publicity has by itself proven an effective weapon in FEP enforcement is not, of course, necessarily an argument for the proposition that it is wholly superfluous to make provision for formal legal sanctions in fair employment legislation. The strategy of enforcement, as far as FEP and other regulatory legislation is concerned, calls for the avoidance of litigation if possible; the coercive effect of publicity may make this possibility a reality. The fact remains, however, that the traditional legal sanctions may also prove indispensable to an FEP agency in dealing with pockets of resistance to the law that are relatively impervious to extra-legal pressures. Both the New York and the Connecticut FEP

settled all but 10 out of 514 cases of probable discrimination (most of them in the area of employment) through conference and conciliation. See New York State Commission against Discrimination. *Annual Report 1959* (New York, 1960), p. 5.

[31] See W. Brooke Graves, *Anti-Discrimination Legislation in the American States* (Washington, 1948).

agencies have found it necessary to call public hearings in connection with trade-union discrimination against Negroes, which in some areas has proved a difficult knot to unravel.

Moreover, an occasional public hearing, so long as the verdict is in its favor, may prove a distinct advantage to an FEP agency as a method of calling attention to itself and its vigilant enforcement of the law. Malcolm Ross, wartime director of the President's Committee on Fair Employment Practice, has called attention to the fact that the national agency's success in disposing of complaints without formal hearings or publicity proved a disadvantage in maintaining public awareness and support of the committee's work.[32] It is, however, this very desire for publicity concerning enforcement vigilance that may push a regulatory agency, no more FEP than any other, into unwarranted prosecutions. This danger is especially acute when an active and vociferous clientele clamors for action on the part of officials charged with responsibility for enforcing the law. At least two observers have commented upon the intense pressure in this direction that has been exerted upon the New York FEP agency.[33]

One impressive indication of the importance of publicity as a sanction in administrative adjudication may be found in the so-called Lamb case, which came before the Federal Communications Commission in 1953.[34] This case grew out of the refusal of the FCC to act favorably on a request for a license renewal by Edward O. Lamb, owner of a television station in Erie, Pennsylvania. As it subsequently developed, the FCC's action in this case was based upon derogatory information it had received linking Lamb with Communist or subversive ac-

[32] See *All Manner of Men* (New York, 1948), pp. 39–40.

[33] See Ruchames, *op. cit.*, pp. 171–77, and Morroe Berger, *Equality by Statute* (New York, 1952), pp. 153–56.

[34] For a report on the Lamb case I am indebted to a paper prepared by Nelson W. Polsby for a graduate seminar in public administration at The Johns Hopkins University. The FCC examiner eventually ruled in Lamb's favor. See, in this regard, *New York Times,* December 8, 1955, p. 24.

tivities. Throughout this case, from its inception to its conclusion, the battle between Lamb and the FCC was waged as much in the newspapers and trade journals as in the hearing room. In an effort to combat the unfavorable publicity resulting from FCC press releases on the charges against Lamb, his lawyers took ads in newspapers and filed suits and charges against the FCC alleging defamation of character and, among other things, the bribery of witnesses. If this case represents a trend the press release is as important a weapon in adversary proceedings before regulatory agencies as the legal brief, and newspaper publicity will come to occupy more of an attorney's attention than trial strategy.

Noteworthy in this case, of course, is the fact that Lamb, owner of three television stations and otherwise a wealthy man, was able to match government publicity broadside for broadside. Equally fortunate was Bernard Goldfine, the New England industrialist and friend of several high government officials (including Presidential Assistant Sherman Adams). When Goldfine was under investigation by a House Committee in 1958, he hired a public relations adviser, Tex McCrary, to assist him in preparing his public defense. McCrary went so far as to write in stage directions in the statement prepared for his client's delivery before the House committee. It hardly needs mentioning that not many private individuals would be in a financial position to employ such talented assistance.

Government and Tobacco

One group that has gone to considerable length to combat unfavorable government publicity is the tobacco industry. In January of 1954 fourteen of the leading tobacco distributors organized a "Tobacco Industry Research Committee" to investigate the causes of lung cancer, a disease that at that time was being increasingly linked to cigarette smoking. The Committee immediately took full page ads in leading newspapers across the country to deny that there was any substantial proof that smoking actually caused lung cancer and announced that it was launching a program of research designed to discover the real causes of the disease. Dr. Clarence C. Little, an internationally known cancer scientist, was appointed chairman of a scientific advisory board to the committee, and by 1959 the group had awarded over $3,000,000 in research grants.

During the first years of its existence the committee concentrated a great deal of its efforts upon counteracting statements issued by private individuals and organizations which attempted to relate smoking and lung cancer. The American Cancer Society was perhaps the chief thorn in the committee's flesh in this regard, but it also had occasion to issue a press release refuting reports which linked smoking to lung cancer that were delivered at meetings of organizations such as the American Medical and the American Public Health Associations. It was not until June of 1955 that the committee was obliged to deal with official government publicity which identified smoking with lung cancer. At that time it issued a report scoring a suggestion by the Census Bureau that a recent drop in cigarette smoking was due to fear of lung cancer. Up until then the government had not itself been directly involved in the controversy over smoking and lung cancer, in spite of the feeling, prevalent in some quarters, that the agencies concerned with public health should take a forthright position on this subject.

Finally, however, in June of 1955 the National Cancer Institute released a report indicating that there appeared to be a definite relationship between smoking and lung cancer. Even as this announcement was being reported, however, the newspapers carried a rebuttal from the tobacco research committee which took sharp issue with the findings of the cancer institute:

> Statisticians and experimental scientists have questioned previously published statistical studies and have pointed out that mathematical correlations do not demonstrate a cause and effect relationship.
> The Tobacco Industry Research Committee is sponsoring a wide range of active research by independent scientists in this area of interest, having so far allocated $1,500,000 for this work.[35]

Here, as on other occasions, the tobacco institute was able to soften the impact of an official government release by having its rebuttal contained in the same news stories which carried the official government announcement.

In July, 1957, the Public Health Service took the official position that there was "increasing and consistent evidence" that excessive cigarette smoking is one of the causative factors of lung cancer. At the same time the Surgeon-General announced the beginning of an educational campaign alerting the public to the dangers of smoking. Copies of the Public Health report were sent to public health officers in each of the states as well as to the American Medical Association. From the tobacco research committee there came an immediate statement from Dr. Little, arguing that the Surgeon-General's pronouncement had added nothing new but had merely restated the views of the "relatively few experimental scientists who have actively charged that cigarette smoking is the cause of lung cancer." Throughout this dispute, the tobacco industry has taken the position that the mere discovery of a statistical correlation between smoking and lung cancer is itself of little significance, a view which may serve its interests but hardly endears it to students of biometrics.

There has been some criticism of the industry for the so-called propaganda it has carried on through its tobacco re-

[35] *New York Times,* June 17, 1956, p. 38.

search committee.[36] Insofar, however, as this criticism is directed at the honest efforts of the tobacco industry to defend itself against adverse publicity, it does not seem warranted. Although the industry's attempts to disparage the importance of statistical findings are purely self-serving, they are well within the bounds of propriety, at least as long as the experts are themselves in disagreement as to the exact relationship between smoking and lung cancer. What is rather to be deplored is the fact that not every individual has similar resources with which to defend himself against charges damaging to a reputation if not an economic asset.

Much more reprehensible, if true, is the accusation that the tobacco companies have brought pressure to bear against certain media of communication to prevent the airing of evidence that smoking does in fact cause lung cancer. The advertising firm of Batten, Barton, Durstine and Osborne, for example, canceled its advertising account with the *Reader's Digest* after that journal published an article showing the ineffectiveness of filter tips on cigarettes for removing the tar and nicotine suspected of causing cancer, and it has been alleged that this action was taken under pressure from one of the firm's principal customers, the American Tobacco Company.[37] Here the industry can be charged not with attempting to get its own point of view before the public, but with stifling the opportunity for contrary opinions to be heard. But in appraising the activities of the industry in this respect, we have at this point only conjecture and rumor to go on.

The Scope of Control

The effectiveness of governmental publicity as a technique of punishment turns almost entirely on the extent to which

[36] See, for example, the letter in the *New York Times* by Professor John K. Galbraith, August 19, 1959, p. 28.

[37] *New York Times*, July 18, 1957, p. 41.

those against whom it is applied are themselves subject to the force of public opinion. Insofar as it can be shown, for example, that current developments in social and economic organization reinforce the tendency of private individuals to avoid unpleasant public notice whenever possible, then it can reasonably be predicted that governmental use of publicity will acquire increased importance in law enforcement as time goes on. For as noted earlier, it is a chief characteristic of publicity as an official control technique that it derives its impact from factors that are very largely beyond governmental determination.

As important as any aspect of the publicity sanction is the fact that it is subject to such sizeable variations in its effectiveness against different individuals. In this respect, publicity is not of course singular, since it is in the nature of punishments to vary in their real as distinguished from their nominal effect. Imprisonment, for example, may represent separation from life for some individuals, while, for others, it offers separation from anxiety. But the variability of the publicity sanction goes even deeper than this. It has indeed no uniform dimensions comparable to a term of years or the sum of dollars usually applied as legal penalties.

This lack of uniformity in its impact is largely traceable to the intangibility of publicity as a punishment. Curiously enough, it is from this amorphous quality that publicity derives both its greatest weakness and its greatest strength as a method of governmental coercion. In some cases in which it may be used, publicity may represent no punishment at all. Indeed some individuals may even aspire to the notoriety connected with violations of what they consider to be obnoxious laws. During World War II, Sewell Avery, the head of Montgomery Ward, made an ostentatious display of his defiance of the orders of the War Labor Board, going as far on one occasion as to allow himself to be lifted bodily from the firm's

Chicago office by two soldiers rather than submit to an order of the board. Later, he said that he had undergone this apparent humiliation in order to dramatize "the march of dictatorship" in the United States.[38]

Other persons, however, may not even be able to envisage the upper limits of adverse publicity as a form of punishment. Some individuals may in fact over-react to the threat of unpleasant notoriety—may have a fear of publicity as inflicting damage far out of proportion to its real impact. This may be the situation today in states which have fair employment practice laws. Just as employers once entertained exaggerated expectations of adverse public reaction to the employment of members of certain minority groups, so they may now be mistaken in expecting public obloquy if they are even charged with discrimination. We are thus confronted with the fact that fear of adverse public reaction, which once acted to prevent the employment of Negroes, can now serve in some parts of the North to encourage it.

Among the factors determining the punitive or coercive effect of publicity as used by government, two may be said to be of central importance. The first of these is the depth of public odium attached to behavior against which the sanction is directed. The second is the importance attached to being in good public repute by the person or institution against which the sanction is threatened or imposed.

Thus, developments in society that increase the degree of odium attached to a particular kind of behavior may increase the impact of publicity as a sanction against acts in this category. This follows from the fact, previously noted, that the publicity sanction must ultimately be inflicted by the public itself. Similarly, developments that heighten individual sensitivity to the opinions of others, whether the general public or some more specific segment of the community, strengthen

[38] *New York Times*, June 7, 1944, p. 21.

the susceptibility of the persons concerned to governmental control through adverse publicity. Since publicity does not represent actual physical coercion, the person against whom the sanction is used must, in some sense at least, allow himself to be constrained by it.

The Impact of Public Opinion

As far as the influence of public opinion upon the punitive character of the publicity sanction is concerned, it has of course long been recognized that law in books cannot be enforced in the absence of public support of law in action. It is this fact that has made use of publicity much more effective in some areas of administrative regulation than in others. The Federal Trade Commission's enforcement of the norm of competition upon business has been more than handicapped by public apathy and even hostility toward its pursuit of this objective. However, as indicated earlier, the experience of other regulatory agencies has been quite different in character, as for example those agencies involved in the regulation of the securities market or the banking system.

This is not to imply, however, that any agency deals in its enforcement program with a fixed structure of public opinion. It is in fact the malleability of opinion regarding an agency's program that gives a special importance to the opinion-shaping activities of regulatory agencies. Although the public relations activity of some administrative agencies may be described as purely informational and educational in character, this can hardly be said to be the case with regulatory agencies. To the extent that this activity widens public understanding and appreciation of the agency's goals, it helps structure an unfavorable public attitude toward those found in violation of the statutes administered by the agency. The creation of such an attitude strengthens the agency's ability to use the threat of adverse publicity as a coercive device to enforce compliance with the law.

Moreover, there may be situations in which such publicity may serve to widen the scope of an agency's powers beyond the boundaries fixed by statute. Both public pronouncements by administrative officials and the issuance of official publications by administrative agencies may accomplish this extra-legal extension of power. Kenneth Davis has pointed out, for example, that the control exercised over the communications industry by the FCC has been sizeably broadened in this informal way by means of speeches delivered by members of the commission and through publication of an official manual containing a formal enunciation of the policies and standards followed by the commission in its regulatory task. As Davis puts it: "The regulation in all these instances was fully effective, even though the Commission conducted no proceeding, took no evidence, afforded no opportunity for cross-examination or submittal of rebuttal evidence, listened to no oral arguments, found no facts, and issued no formal rule." [39]

One of the handicaps under which economic regulation has traditionally labored has been the tendency of the public to look with less disfavor upon offenses against laws regulating economic behavior than it does upon violations of ordinary criminal statutes.[40] Consequently, persons subject to such regulation have been threatened with less public stigma for violations than, by comparison, has been visited upon those caught in the net of traditional law enforcement. It is, of course, true that a business firm ordinarily commands publicity resources that enable it to counteract adverse governmental publicity,

[39] Kenneth C. Davis, *Administrative Law Treatise* (St. Paul, 1958), Vol. I, p. 245.
[40] For a discussion of the relationship between public opinion and law enforcement in this respect, see Edwin H. Sutherland, *White Collar Crime* (New York, 1949); and Clinard, *op. cit.*, Chaps. 4, 11.

and this fact alone would make publicity less effective as a sanction against an economic enterprise than it might be against a private individual.

In part, however, the lesser degree of disgrace attached to white collar crime is a product of the traditional American commitment to freedom from governmental interference with private economic activity. In societies based upon collective rather than individual conduct of economic activities, whether primitive or modern socialized economies, deviance from approved norms of economic behavior may expect to encounter much more severe public disapproval. Consequently, if, as presently appears to be the case, public opinion in this country is moving toward greater acceptance of public control of private economic activity, violations of economic regulatory statutes can expect to encounter increased public disfavor in the future. At the same time, moreover, the publicity sanction will come to acquire increased power as a coercive device in governmental regulation, and the need for providing protection against its abuse will take on correspondingly increased importance.

Sensitivity to Publicity

The sensitivity of individuals and institutions to coercion by publicity is, like the public attitude toward sanctioned activity, subject to a good deal of variation. Evidence on the factors that lead to differences in the degree to which people are subject to such control is quite fragmentary, and any discussion of the subject must necessarily be exploratory in character. However, although this problem may very well have immeasurable aspects, it would also seem that further empirical research would turn up evidence on the dimensions of the variables determining both susceptibility and resistance to control by the publicity sanction, as well as throw light upon the interrelationships prevailing among these factors.

This is not to minimize the complexity of the problem. Off-hand, for example, it might be assumed that a business firm enjoying something of a monopoly would be less subject to control by publicity in economic regulation than a firm in a competitive industry. A monopoly would have comparatively little to fear from the adverse opinion of a public that has only limited alternatives to purchase of its product. Not only would a firm in a competitive industry be in no such secure economic position, but it could well anticipate that news of any mis-demeanor in which it was involved would be advertised far and wide by its competitors. Contrary considerations that need, however, to be taken into account in any analysis of this economic factor include the fact that some of the firms in a competitive situation are marginal firms, driven perhaps to ignore all such intangible factors as public opinion in the pur-suit of survival itself. Moreover, a monopoly may have more to fear from government regulation or competition than a firm in a competitive industry and hence may be more inter-ested in cultivating the good will of the public as a defense against restrictive legislation.[41]

One group of authors has also suggested that the prestige of the agency administering the sanction has a great deal to do with the effectiveness of publicity as a method of control: "The prestige of the administrative agency involved is a fac-tor, as is the prestige of the enterprise against which the sanc-tion is employed. Publicity by any agency, however weak, is a stronger weapon against the established and reputable

[41] Robert E. Lane, *The Regulation of Businessmen* (New Haven, 1954), Chap. 5, contains an interesting analysis of some other factors that account for differing degrees of respect accorded regulatory statutes by businessmen. His-torically it was of course monopolistic enterprise that pioneered in public relations activity. See, in this connection, Norton Long, "Public Relations Policies of the Bell System," *Public Opinion Quarterly*, Vol. I (October, 1937), pp. 5–22.

enterprise than it is against the ephemeral and disreputable. But publicity by a weak agency or an agency weakened by a concerted campaign is comparatively ineffectual even against established and reputable enterprises." [42]

It may be the case that, as far as a business firm is concerned, the style rather than the extent of competition in which it is involved is the central factor determining its susceptibility to control by publicity. A firm engaged in product differentiation rather than price competition is selling a reputation, fictional perhaps, but a reputation nonetheless. Under such circumstances the slightest breath of unfavorable publicity may loom as a dire peril. The well-known sensitivity to adverse publicity of advertising companies, marketing agents for firms engaged in product differentiation, is perhaps the best indication of the relationship between this style of competition and susceptibility to publicity as a method of control.

Insofar, at least, as the institutionalization of the public relations function occurs only in firms of relatively large size, there may also be said to be a positive correlation between size of firm and sensitivity to governmental control by the publicity sanction. This assumes that with the employment of a public relations specialist, a firm undertakes a decisive commitment to give public relations considerations important standing in its decision-making process. A corollary assumption is, of course, that the introduction of a specific spokesman for public relations considerations into the executive hierarchy results in a significant increment being added to the influence of the public relations factor in policy decisions.

The quest for favorable publicity signalled by the employment by business firms and other institutions of public relations counselors is in part an attempt to avoid the obvious economic penalties that may follow in the wake of adverse public attention, such as a reduction in sales. In part also, it is

[42] Chamberlain, Dowling, and Hays, *op. cit.*, p. 112.

a product of the desire to establish and maintain more subtle assets such as respectability and prestige in the eyes of the community. The manner in which these psychological and economic incentives to avoid adverse publicity are woven together is difficult to determine, but it is at least likely that they reinforce as well as relate to each other.

It is in any event clear that whether it be traceable to an increasing tendency toward monopoly in the American economy, or the increasing resort to product differentiation as a style of competition, or even the increase in the size of firms and the growth in the employment of public relations experts, the fact of the matter is that business firms, and other social institutions as well, exhibit far more sensitivity to adverse publicity today than would have been the case a few decades ago. There have been few transformations in American life as sharp as the shift in the attitude of business from one of indifference to that of preoccupation with the character of public sentiment toward itself.[43] This development has very frequently been noted in connection with the growing sense of public responsibility evident in such recent patterns of business behavior as the conduct of employee welfare programs. That its assiduous cultivation of public good will increases the susceptibility of business to government control by publicity is also clear.

An attempt has been made in this chapter to indicate some elements in social and economic development and organization that help to account for the power of publicity as a method of restraint in governmental hands. As important, perhaps, as any of the factors that have been singled out for examination is this growing public relations mindedness on the part of institutions and individuals. To the extent that this desire for

---

[43] See the discussion of the contemporary influence of public opinion upon corporations and corporate executives in A. A. Berle, Jr., *The Twentieth Century Capitalist Revolution* (New York, 1954), especially pp. 54–60.

public esteem leads to growing pressure for the avoidance of all criticism, however unjust and whatever its source, this emerging public relations orientation may result in a notable increase in the strain toward conformity in American society. In this event, there may well be future occasion for nostalgia, on the part at least of those partisan to independence of outlook, for the "public-be-damned" attitude of the traditional entrepreneur.

CHAPTER 7

PUBLICITY AND THE LAW

OF FUNDAMENTAL importance in any constitutional society is the requirement that a technique of government control be subject to limitations that will prevent its being used in an arbitrary or unjustified way. In this respect government control through publicity opens up novel and perplexing problems in our society, mainly because the American constitutional system is geared to protecting the rights of individuals against the formal prosecuting power of government, whereas the use of publicity represents an informal method of constraint of a kind that does not easily lend itself to definition or control within formal legal categories.

As is customary in American politics with problems of this kind, the task of striking a balance between the protection of private rights and the necessary and proper use of publicity in government regulation has mainly been left in the hands of the judiciary. The responsibility delegated to the courts is not of course an exclusive one. The legislature through its jurisdiction over its own rules of procedure, especially as they pertain to the operations of its committees, and its ability to fix and alter the procedures of executive agencies, itself has the capacity, largely untapped, to do much to adjudicate the competing claims of freedom and control in this area of the law. Administrative agencies, acting within their own discretionary powers, can also exert a similar though lesser influence, and, as already noted, regulatory agencies have commonly adopted restraints upon the use of publicity in law enforcement.[1] Nevertheless, it is the judiciary that has been left to grapple most directly with the task of reconciling control through publicity with the ways of democracy.

Defamation by Government Officials

It is, therefore, of no small importance that the courts, in their handling of this problem, have exhibited an extreme reluctance to set sharp limits to governmental use of publicity that might result in coercion or damage to private persons. This has been true even when a showing could be made that this official publicity was of rather dubious ethical, if not legal, justification. In, for example, the case of libel suits filed by private citizens against government officials, alleging defamation of character as a result of official publicity, the general rule followed by the courts has been that even though these officials are not granted constitutional immunity against such claims, they should, nevertheless, be afforded wide protection against liability even for maliciously inspired damage to private reputation.

Thus, the courts long ago granted cabinet officials an absolute immunity from libel similar to that enjoyed by congress-

---

[1] As pointed out in Chapter 3, one of the principal factors accounting for the growth of administrative secrecy has been a desire on the part of regulatory agencies to shield private parties from unpleasant publicity. In the study of the regulatory process by Chamberlain, Dowling and Hays, *The Judicial Function in Federal Administrative Agencies* (New York, 1942), it is noted that agencies such as the Department of Agriculture in its administration of the Grain Standards Act and the Federal Deposit Insurance Corporation have long followed a policy of internal restraint on use of the publicity sanction for precisely this reason.

men under the Constitution. As early as 1896 the Supreme Court ruled that the postmaster-general was protected by such immunity notwithstanding the fact that he may have been motivated by malice in including statements damaging to the reputation of a private citizen in an official communication of the department.[2] An administrator, the Court declared, "should not be under an apprehension that the motives that control his official conduct may at any time become the subject of inquiry in a civil suit for damages."

This precedent has been followed by the Court in subsequent decisions. In one of the more famous cases, *Glass* v. *Ickes*, the Court extended the immunity afforded cabinet officials against libel suits to include statements made in press releases.[3] In this case Ickes as Secretary of the Interior was judged absolutely immune from a libel suit whether or not he had, as alleged, defamed Glass by innuendo in a press release implying that the inability of Glass to practice as an attorney before the Department of the Interior reflected some special misconduct on his part. The disbarment concerned had in fact been one automatically applied to Glass and all others who had worked for the department during the preceding two-year period. In expressing his reluctant concurrence with this decision on the basis of precedents, Chief Justice Groner of the Court of Appeals nevertheless stated: "I express with great deference the fear that in this and previous cases we may have extended the rule beyond the reasons out of which it grew and thus unwittingly created a privilege so extensive as to be almost unlimited and altogether subversive of the fundamental principle that no man in this country is so high that he is above the law."

    [2] *Spalding* v. *Vilas*, 161 U.S. 483 (1896).
    [3] 117 F. 2d 273 (1940). Other decisions include *Matson* v. *Margiotti*, 371 Pa. 188, 88 A. 2d 892 (1952); *Miles* v. *McGrath*, 4 F. Supp. 603 (1933); *United States* v. *Birdsall*, 233 U.S. 223 (1914). For an argument that the immunity from libel presently enjoyed by executive officials is far too extensive, see Comment, "Defamation Immunity for Executive Officers," *University of Chicago Law Review*, Vol. 20 (Summer, 1953), pp. 677–92.

In the Glass and in other cases, the courts have also followed the earlier Spalding decision in giving protection to a very wide range of statements by a cabinet officer, including, as permitted by the Spalding ruling, pronouncements having only "more or less connection with the general matters committed by law" to his discretion. Justification for the ample latitude thus given to the possible misuse of official power has been found in the fact that such immunity frees departmental officials from the threat of harassment by civil suits, thus enabling them to discharge their public functions in an uninhibited and competent manner. In no other way, the courts have reasoned, can the public interest in the efficient conduct of governmental affairs be maintained.

Moreover, the European experience suggests the possibility that, in the absence of judicial restraint, libel suits might well be used by totalitarian political groups to harass and intimidate public officials from acting against them in a democracy. This was a tactic used with considerable success by the Nazi party during the days of the Weimar Republic in Germany, when libel suits were filed by Hitler and other Nazi officials in an effort to silence criticism of the party and its leaders. And David Riesman has pointed out that in this country there was at least some beginning toward using the libel suit during the thirties as part of "a reactionary campaign, Nazi-style, against democratic criticism." [4] This same practice has also been followed by Communist parties. (Its effectiveness in this country would be much reduced by the absence of group libel statutes.)

The courts have also been influenced in the protection they have given executive officials against libel suits by the consideration that if the public is properly to direct and supervise the work of administrative agencies, it must have full information

[4] David Riesman, "Democracy and Defamation: Fair Game and Fair Comment I," *Columbia Law Review*, Vol. 42 (Sept., 1942), p. 1090.

regarding the problems which confront public officials. Judicial imposition of restraints upon government publicity, even if intended merely to protect the reputation of private citizens from unnecessary damage, might very well have a constricting effect upon government by discussion. The dilemma with which the courts have been faced is, as stated in one case, that "whatever is added to the field of libel is taken from the field of free debate." [5]

Two recent cases decided by the Supreme Court point up the fact that this dilemma is still with us. For as the Court noted in handing down its opinion in one of these controversies: "We are called upon in this case to weigh in a particular context two considerations of high importance which now and again come into sharp conflict—on the one hand, the protection of the individual citizen against pecuniary damage caused by oppressive or malicious action on the part of officials of the Federal Government; and on the other, the protection of the public interest by shielding responsible governmental officers against the harassment and inevitable hazards of vindictive or ill-founded damage suits brought on account of action taken in the exercise of their official responsibilities." [6]

One of these cases, *Barr* v. *Matteo*, grew out of a libel suit brought by two former employees of the Office of Rent Stabilization against the acting director of that agency, who had issued a press release holding the employees responsible for a fiscal procedure the agency had followed which was widely criticized by Congress and the press in 1953. This was the practice of paying certain employees accrued annual leave as terminal leave, and then discharging and rehiring them as temporary employees. It was variously referred to on the floor of

---

[5] *Sweeney* v. *Patterson*, 128 F. 2d 457 (1942). This case involved defamation of, rather than by, a government official.

[6] *Barr* v. *Matteo*, 360 U.S. 564 (1959).

Congress as "a raid on the Federal Treasury," "a conspiracy to defraud the Government of funds," and a "new racket." Ultimately, however, the Court of Claims decided that it was within the letter of the law, even if, from the point of view of some observers, its ethics might be questionable.

Both the district and the Appeals Court upheld the two employees in their contention that they had been defamed. The Court of Appeals ruled that the director of the agency had gone outside the line of duty in issuing his press release, and it rested its opinion in part upon the belief that the absolute privilege against libel enunciated in earlier decisions did not apply to officials of so subordinate a rank. But when the case was taken before the Supreme Court, these contentions were rejected. In an opinion by Justice Harlan, the Court reaffirmed the right of the agency director to issue the press release in question and dismissed the libel suit.

In dealing with the claim that the director went outside the bounds of his official authority in issuing such a press release the Court noted that,

> The issuance of press releases was standard agency practice, as it has become with many governmental agencies in these times. We think that under these circumstances a publicly expressed statement of the position of the agency head, announcing personnel action which he planned to take in reference to the charges so widely disseminated to the public, was an appropriate exercise of the discretion which an officer of that rank must possess if the public service is to function effectively. It would be an unduly restrictive view of the scope of the duties of a policy-making executive official to hold that a public statement of agency policy in respect to matters of wide public interest and concern is not action in the line of duty.

The Court was equally emphatic in rejecting the argument that the privilege of executive immunity from libel should be confined to high-ranking officials.

The privilege is not a badge or emolument of exalted office, but an expression of a policy designed to aid in the effective functioning of government. The complexities and magnitude of governmental activity have become so great that there must of necessity be a delegation and redelegation of authority as to many functions, and we cannot say that these functions become less important simply because they are exercised by officers of lower rank in the executive hierarchy.

In a concurring opinion, Justice Black also advanced the argument that the ability of government officials to issue press releases is essential to the general task of informing the public as to the quality of government service.

Chief Justice Warren and Justice Douglas entered a strong dissent from the opinion of the Court in this case. They asserted that the Court, in extending the privilege of immunity from libel to cover subordinate as well as high ranking executive officials, had seriously inhibited the right of the public to speak out against official policy:

. . . here the Court has given some amorphous group of officials —who have the most direct and personal contact with the public —an absolute privilege when their agency or their action is criticized. In this situation, it will take a brave person to criticize government officials knowing that in reply they may libel him with immunity in the name of defending the agency and their own position. This extension of *Spalding* v. *Vilas* can only have the added effect of deterring the desirable public discussion of all aspects of our Government and the conduct of its officials. It will sanctify the powerful and silence debate.

This argument put heavy weight on the fact that the Court now gave public officials an absolute immunity from libel which had always been denied to private citizens who criticized the acts of government officials.

Justice Brennan expressed similar fears in dissenting from the decision of the Court handed down the same day in a companion case, *Howard* v. *Lyons*.[7] Brennan argued that a qualified privilege is all that it is necessary to give government officials in cases of this kind—a privilege that would protect an official "unless it appeared on trial that his communication was (a) defamatory, (b) untrue, and (c) 'malicious.' " For, as Brennan noted, "a qualified privilege would be the most the law would allow private citizens under comparable circumstances." It was Brennan's suggestion that if any serious inconvenience to the executive should result from a system of qualified rather than absolute immunity from libel, Congress could easily amend the Tort Claims Act so that the government itself rather than any particular official would pay the damages awarded in court to any private citizen who won a defamation suit. This is one of the most constructive suggestions that has yet come out of the judicial debate over executive publicity.

Exposure through Adjudication

The punitive effect of publicity initiated by governmental action has also been brought to judicial attention in connection with suits seeking injunctive relief from the adverse publicity threatened by pending administrative proceedings. However, the courts have been just as reluctant to grant relief of this kind as they have been to sustain libel actions against government officials. In one case, involving the Federal Trade Commission, a business firm put forth the claim that the mere announcement in trade journals of a forthcoming hearing involving the firm had damaged its business, and that an actual public hearing on the matter would "aggravate and increase the injury," for which there was no adequate remedy at common law.[8] In dis-

[7] 360 U.S. 593 (1959).
[8] *E. Griffiths Hughes, Inc.* v. *Federal Trade Commission*, 63 F. 2d, 362 (1933).

missing this complaint, an appeals court gave as its opinion that the firm would actually have been in a far worse position if the FTC had been allowed to hold hearings in private. Said the court: "The purpose underlying the constitutional guaranty of public trial in prosecutions for crime is to prevent abuses arising out of the avarice of unprincipled officials or the sale of justice or a conviction through illegal evidence. The rule requiring public hearings, whether in courts or bureaus, avoids these possibilities, and is to be approved." While the court here refused to grant an injunction for the protection of so intangible an asset as a firm's reputation when "the possibility of loss is founded wholly on the public knowledge that an investigation has been ordered," it did suggest that where such tangible assets as trade secrets are jeopardized by publicity, injunctive relief might be available under the law.

In *Myers* v. *Bethlehem Shipbuilding Corporation*, it was decided that injunctive relief from adverse governmental publicity could not be granted even though an executive agency may have exceeded its authority in taking jurisdiction over a case.[9] Such relief was held similarly unavailable in *Arrow Distilleries* v. *Alexander*, a case in which the claim was made that the statute under which unfavorable publicity was being inflicted was unconstitutional.[10] The basic difficulty faced by litigants in this situation is that the judiciary will not consider a plea for an injunction until all administrative remedies have been exhausted, and it is from the publicity connected with these very administrative "remedies" that an appellant is seeking protection.

The rulings of the judiciary in cases involving administrative adjudication point up the fact that the reluctance of the courts to protect private persons from what may perhaps be the undeserved brunt of unfavorable publicity springs not only

[9] 303 U.S. 41 (1938).
[10] 24 Fed. Supp. 880 (1938).

from the consideration, already discussed, that full disclosure of governmental affairs is important to the preservation of public control over policy-making, but also from the knowledge that this publicity may be indispensable for the protection of private rights. Thus secrecy at the early stages of a proceeding in which he is involved may save an individual from some initial adverse publicity. However, insofar as it serves to mask arbitrary procedures by government officials, such secrecy may ultimately contribute to the imposition of undeserved legal sanctions upon the defendant when the proceeding is concluded. As the Supreme Court once pointed out:

> Whatever other benefits the guarantee to an accused that his trial be conducted in public may confer upon our society, the guarantee has always been recognized as a safeguard against any attempt to employ our courts as instruments of persecution. The knowledge that every criminal trial is subject to contemporaneous review in the forum of public opinion is an effective restraint upon the possible abuse of judicial power.[11]

In their thinking on this matter, the courts have, therefore, been principally impressed with the danger of injustice to a defendant resulting from secrecy rather than the publicity connected with a law enforcement proceeding. For this concern the judiciary can of course find ample support in history. Secrecy has traditionally been a distinctive characteristic of law enforcement in despotic states. However, styles change, in the field of tyranny as elsewhere, and publicity could in its own way become as much a source of injustice as secrecy ever has been. To this point at least, judicial supervision of legislative and executive law enforcement activities has been much more effective in providing protection against secrecy in proceedings of this kind than it has against unwarranted damage resulting from adverse governmental publicity.

[11] *In re Oliver*, 333 U.S. 257 (1948); quoted in Kenneth C. Davis, *Administrative Law Treatise* (St. Paul, 1958), Vol. I, p. 551.

From the point of view of a government official bent upon inflicting the maximum amount of damage, the ideal situation is one in which he can manipulate the proper "mix" of publicity and secrecy so that each helps to put a defendant at a disadvantage, since public opinion in any society is a function both of what is known and what is not known. During the investigation conducted by the Senate Committee on Government Operations into alleged subversion at Fort Monmouth, for example, Senator McCarthy, the chairman of the committee, made a regular practice of hearing witnesses in executive session, only to issue forth at the end of each day's secret proceedings with an *ex parte* bulletin on what the testimony had revealed. Newspapers across the country carried lurid headlines on the horrendous implications of the testimony about Fort Monmouth—implications that were not at all borne out many months later when the full transcript of the committee hearings was finally made public.

> The whole thing was a shameless case of synthetic publicity-seeking, carried out with no regard for the facts or the national welfare. Eventually, of course, the press was able to penetrate closer to the shabby truth, but in the meantime great harm had been done both to the Signal Corps and to individuals.[12]

A similarly disadvantageous mixture of governmental secrecy and publicity may confront a government employee charged with the necessity of defending himself against the charge of being a security risk. Such matters as the identity of the source of derogatory information may, to the disadvantage of the employee, be kept from him, while at the same time ex-

---

[12] Telford Taylor, *Grand Inquest* (New York, 1955), p. 246. The legality of the Senator's behavior in this case was subsequently upheld by the New Jersey Supreme Court, *Coleman* v. *Newark Morning Star Ledger Co.*, 149 A. 2d 193 (1959). This case grew out of the unsuccessful efforts of one witness before McCarthy's committee to recover damages from a Newark newspaper for stories carried by the paper which—on the basis of McCarthy press conference statements—linked the witness with an atom spy ring.

posure to his colleagues and perhaps to the public as a security risk may inflict on him the full weight of adverse opinion. To be sure, such exposure must ordinarily come from leaks or gossip, since executive procedures have themselves provided for privacy on loyalty-security hearings.

Loyalty and Publicity

Reluctant as the courts traditionally have been to consider adverse publicity as one of the governmental sanctions against which private individuals are entitled to judicial relief, recent years have seen increasing pressure exerted upon the judiciary to revise its thinking on this score. This pressure has come in the main from individuals claiming immunity or injury from one or another of the extensive efforts undertaken by all the instruments of law enforcement since World War II to control and punish subversive activities. In at least one respect this pressure has had a fate different from previous efforts to convince the courts that a judicial remedy ought to be provided against unjust use of the publicity sanction. Individuals aggrieved by governmental publicity linking them with subversive activities have had a good deal more success in convincing the courts that a real and very punitive sanction has been imposed upon them than litigants claiming damage from governmental publicity in other connections.[13] Cloistered though they may be, the courts have had little difficulty sensing the depth and in-

---

[13] The courts have not always shown complete awareness of the conditions under which adverse publicity may impose a penalty in economic regulation. Judicial decisions in such cases have tended to underestimate the extent to which derogatory publicity concerning a business firm may inflict damage even if restricted in its circulation to a small group. This can occur when the firm is economically dependent upon the good will of the group concerned for its livelihood. See the discussion of "defamation and public opinion" in David Riesman, "Democracy and Defamation: Fair Game and Fair Comment," *op. cit.*, pp. 1085–1123, 1282–1318, especially pp. 1300–1308.

tensity of public antipathy toward "un-American activities" and the odium and consequent penalties attached to public exposure of an individual as a subversive.[14]

While generally agreeing that, as far as its capacity to identify individuals with subversion is concerned, publicity in governmental hands can be a sanction with great punitive effect, judges have disagreed, sometimes quite sharply, as to whether this puts any obligation upon the courts to restrain such governmental publicity. In the field of legislative investigations, for example, the courts have rejected the claim that congressional inquiries into the affiliations of individuals with subversive organizations are unconstitutional because they threaten individuals and groups identified as subversive with the penalty of adverse publicity and thus interfere with the freedom of speech and association guaranteed by the First Amendment. The argument here has been that what Congress cannot punish by legislation, it cannot punish by exposure. In *United States* v. *Josephson* the court dismissed this argument, saying that the Constitution does not protect the "timidity" of individuals fearful of unfavorable publicity, and that, as far as any threat to the individual and his freedom of speech from the publicity sanction is concerned, "until there is a valid law to the contrary, he may with impunity say what he pleases *so far as legal process is concerned*, and that is the extent of the freedom of speech guaranteed anyone by the Constitution." [15]

In *Barsky* v. *United States* the Court of Appeals for the District of Columbia rejected a similar contention put forward in an appeal against conviction for contempt of Congress, where it was alleged that "since an answer that the witness is a Communist would subject him to embarrassment and damage, the asking of the question is an unconstitutional burden upon

[14] One of the best measures of this antipathy in the period since World War II is to be found in Samuel Stouffer, *Communism, Conformity and Civil Liberties* (New York, 1955).

[15] 165 F. 2d 82 (1947), certiorari denied, 333 U.S. 838 (1948), italics mine.

free speech." [16] While this time conceding that "even the most timid and sensitive cannot be unconstitutionally restrained in the freedom of his thought," the court nevertheless held that the Communist movement represented a clear and present danger to the national security that would justify inquiry by the House Committee on Un-American Activities into an individual's affiliations with Communist organizations. In an opinion strongly dissenting from this decision, Justice Edgerton of the Court of Appeals declared: "The investigation restricts the freedom of speech by uncovering and stigmatizing expressions of unpopular views. The Committee gives wide publicity to its proceedings. This exposes the men and women whose views are advertised to risks of insult, ostracism, and lasting loss of employment. . . . The Committee's practice of advertising and stigmatizing unpopular views is therefore a strong deterrent to any expression, however private, of such views. . . . Some people speak freely whatever it costs, but this does not mean that speech is free whatever it costs. . . . What Congress may not restrain, Congress may not restrain by exposure and obloquy."

The Supreme Court decision which has attracted the greatest public attention to this problem of publicity as a method of punishment in the field of Congressional investigations is *Watkins* v. *United States*, handed down in 1957.[17] Here Chief Justice Warren ruled that there is "no congressional power to expose for the sake of exposure" and that investigations which compel the disclosure of the affairs of private citizens are only valid when they serve a legitimate legislative purpose. In this instance it was held that Watkins, a witness before the House Un-American Affairs Committee, had been given no clear indication of the purpose of the hearing to which he was summoned, nor of the relevance of the questions he was asked to

[16] 167 F. 2d 241 (1948), certiorari denied, 334 U.S. 843 (1948)
[17] 354 U.S. 178 (1957).

any objectives the committee might have in conducting its investigation. Consequently, his refusal to answer some of the questions put to him was justified, and his conviction for contempt of Congress was reversed.

Not all the members of the Court who joined in the Watkins decision were persuaded that the Court's opinion set any limits to the scope of Congress's ability to inflict punishment by publicity. Justice Frankfurter concurred with the Court's opinion purely on the grounds of procedural defects connected with the hearing accorded Watkins. And in an opinion since handed down, *Barenblatt* v. *United States*, the Court itself has expressly disavowed any intention of putting serious restrictions on the congressional power of exposure.[18] As long as an investigation is conducted with procedural regularity, any harmful effects it may have in terms of adverse publicity inflicted upon witnesses called to testify may be regrettable but they are certainly not illegal. This Barenblatt decision aroused sharp dissent from, among others, Justice Brennan, who chided his colleagues with the argument that "an investigation in which the processes of law-making and law evaluating are submerged entirely in exposure of individual behavior—in adjudication of a sort through the exposure process—is outside the constitutional pale of congressional inquiry."

But this view of adverse publicity as a governmental penalty subject to judicial restraint has generally remained a minority view on the bench. For example, Justice Edgerton, of the Court of Appeals for the District of Columbia, who is, as noted above in his decision on the Barsky case, one of the stoutest champions of individual rights as against congressional power, has nonetheless conceded the legislature very substantial latitude in the field of publicity. In *Methodist Federation for Social Action* v. *Eastland,* he ruled that the courts have no power to restrain the publication by Congress of an allegedly defamatory docu-

[18] 360 U.S. 109 (1959).

ment which identified the Methodist Federation as a Com-
munist-front organization, since the congressional immunity
from libel covers publications by Congress as well as floor
statements by congressmen.[19] "We have," he stated, "no more
authority to prevent Congress . . . from publishing a document than to prevent [it] from publishing the *Congressional
Record*. If it unfortunately happens that a document which
Congress has ordered published contains statements that are
erroneous and defamatory, and are made without allowing the
persons affected an opportunity to be heard, this adds nothing
to our authority."

One of the most formidable problems the courts have had to
face in their evaluation of governmental publicity as punishment has arisen out of the operation by the national government of the loyalty-security program covering executive employees. In its administration of this program, set up in 1947
to eliminate and exclude disloyal persons, and since that
time "security risks," from employment in executive agencies,
the government has always taken the position that it is simply
exercising its ordinary and traditional discretion on employment matters when it takes loyalty and security considerations
into account in deciding whom to appoint and whom to exclude from government service. It is settled judicial doctrine
that a government employee does not have a right to his job.
Since an employee can be summarily denied or removed from
a position for a variety of lesser reasons, surely suspicion of
disloyalty provides a reasonable grounds for removal, even if
the procedure used be arbitrary in character. Furthermore,
the government has contended, its moral and legal position in
this connection is made impregnable by the fact that it allows
employees against whom disloyalty charges have been preferred the privilege of a quasi-judicial hearing, even though it
is under no strict constitutional obligation to do so.

[19] 141 F. Supp. 729 (1956).

However persuasive and reasonable this position may be, it has been sharply challenged before the courts by former government employees seeking judicial relief from a finding of disloyalty and subsequent removal from government employment. This challenge has been rooted in the claim that discharge from government service on charges of disloyalty, unlike the other grounds upon which dismissal may occur, inflicts public disgrace upon an individual and opens the door to the application of additional extra-legal sanctions including the denial of private employment. This being the case, it is argued, the government is constitutionally prohibited from discharging an employee for disloyalty except when it follows procedures specified by the Constitution as necessary before any legal punishment can be imposed upon a private citizen. For one thing, the Sixth Amendment of the Constitution prohibits punishment without a fair trial and the requirements of a fair trial, as set forth in the Amendment, include procedures not necessarily followed in the administration of the government's loyalty program—e.g., the accused need not be confronted with the witnesses against him. The constitutional challenge to the loyalty program rests also upon the contention that, contrary to the Fifth Amendment, it takes away liberty and property "without due process of law."

In *Bailey* v. *Richardson*, the Court of Appeals for the District of Columbia considered these rival claims and decided in favor of the government, a ruling in which it was subsequently upheld by the Supreme Court.[20] The Court found itself unable to look upon dismissal from government service as legal punishment, whatever the extra-legal sanctions associated with it might be. Such dismissal was simply denial of a privilege to which no one was legally entitled. As far as the due process clause was concerned, the Court reiterated the oft-stated judicial conviction that no individual has a property right to a

[20] 182 F. 2d 46 (1950), affirmed *per curiam*, 341 U.S. 918 (1951).

government job. "Miss Bailey," the Court pointed out, "may have a perfect right to devote her life to personnel training, but that does not include the right to employment by whatever employer she happens to choose."

The Court's decision in this case may have been the correct one; the public interest in a loyal and efficient civil service may demand that any doubt as to procedural propriety be resolved in favor of the government. But right or wrong as the ruling may have been, the notion of punishment maintained in the Bailey decision is highly formalistic and not entirely supported by judicial precedent. In the Lovett case the Supreme Court took cognizance of the punitive stigma attached to dismissal from an executive agency for disloyalty and provided judicial relief against an act of Congress inflicting this punishment without judicial trial.[21] A variety of earlier decisions limiting the power to tax likewise evidences judicial recognition of the fact that it is not only through legal prosecution that government punishes or coerces. Marshall's venerable doctrine that "the power to tax involves the power to destroy" might well have provided a point of departure for judicial reassessment of the punitive power of publicity in the modern state.

Moreover, the statement that no one has a property right to

[21] 328 U.S. 303 (1946). Later in *Joint Anti-Fascist Refugee Committee* v *McGrath*, 341 U.S. 123 (1951), the Supreme Court was to agree that a private organization had suffered grievous injury through adverse publicity as a result of being designated as subversive by the attorney-general without a hearing. The meaning of this decision for judicial doctrine on the publicity sanction is, however, vitiated by the fact that no less than five separate and distinct opinions were written in connection with the majority decision. (For a critical scrutiny of this kind of judicial individualism, see Carl B. Swisher, "The Supreme Court—Need for Re-Evaluation," *Virginia Law Review*, Vol. 40 [November, 1954], pp. 837–51.) Another related decision was handed down in *Greene* v. *McElroy*, 360 U.S. 474 (1959), a case involving private employment under government contract. The Court held that "the right to hold specific private employment and to follow a chosen profession free from unreasonable governmental interference comes within the 'liberty' and 'property' concepts of the Fifth Amendment."

a government job, itself true beyond peradventure of doubt, does not dispose of the more difficult question of whether a government employee has a property right to his reputation upon which his employability in any position, public or private, may depend. However, in order to deal with this problem the Court would have had to take into account a fairly complex set of considerations, including the extent to which this country has been moving toward an employee society in which the ability to earn a living through wages or salary has increasingly become the essence of property for most individuals. Also relevant in this connection is the fact that probity of reputation becomes well-nigh indispensable in a society in which personality rather than skill assets become key factors in determining suitability for work in the varied bureaucracies that have come to make up the employment market.[22] In a contemporary discussion of congressional investigations of Communism in Hollywood, it is reported that one of William Faulkner's friends "wailed that he had been tapped by the Un-American Activities Committee, and that this could be his ruin. After the victim had departed, Faulkner observed, '———— don't have to worry none, so long as he writes good.' "[23] Faulkner's view is of course a traditional one, but it may very well have been the measure of his friend's predicament that he was not so much a writer as a literary bureaucrat, as replaceable in what is aptly called the entertainment industry as the scenarios he produced.

In *Peters* v. *Hobby*, which was decided by the Supreme Court in 1955, the punitive character of dismissal from the government service was once again pointed up for the Court's inspection in a case that had its origin in the removal of Dr.

[22] C. Wright Mills, *White Collar* (New York, 1951), is perhaps the best-known analysis of the relationship between employment and personality factors in modern society.

[23] Murray Kempton, *Part of Our Time: Some Monuments and Ruins of the Thirties* (New York, 1955), p. 209.

John Peters on loyalty grounds from a position as part-time consultant to the Federal Security Agency.[24] In this appeal the claim was made that during the three years which had elapsed since the Bailey decision abundant evidence had accumulated that dismissal with a finding of disloyalty was more than a hardship, it was in the legal sense a punishment, since it "ruins the reputation and career of the accused." [25] More than that, it was in this case an intended punishment, since the government chose to stigmatize Dr. Peters as a security risk when it could easily have dispensed with his services by ceasing to call upon him as a consultant. As the reason for the government's choice of action in this matter, the appeal brief pointed to the publicity value attached in the minds of executive officials to finding and discharging as many security risks as possible. In its concluding argument to the Court, the brief stated: "The most fundamental subject of constitutional concern is the life and liberty of the individual. Imprisonment of course does not follow the findings of loyalty boards but the penalties are hardly less severe:—ostracism and impoverishment and the denial of access to one's profession and the society of one's friends." [26] The catalogue of punishments here described bears a striking similarity to the penalties visited upon deviant members of primitive societies.

The Supreme Court did not meet the constitutional issues presented by the Peters case, disposing of it with the ruling that the Loyalty Review Board had exceeded its authority in taking jurisdiction over the case and that its finding of disloyalty with regard to Dr. Peters was, therefore, invalid and should be "expunged from the record." Other tests of the government's loyalty security program have also been disposed of on other than constitutional grounds, and we may expect fur-

[24] 349 U.S. 331 (1955).
[25] Ibid., Brief of Petitioner, p. 10.
[26] Ibid., p. 21.

ther decisions on its legality in the future. However, it should be noted that one of the more subtly coercive aspects of publicity is its ability to deter challenges to what may be considered to be unconstitutional government action, when reasonable expectations exist that such challenges will bring unfavorable public attention to the private litigant seeking judicial relief.

In retrospect it is clear that the unwillingness of the judiciary to impose restraints upon governmental coercion through publicity has been rooted in some very compelling considerations, including the necessity of keeping the public informed of the conduct of governmental business, the need of executive officials to be free from the harassment of civil suits in the discharge of their duties and the right of the legislature to investigate matters within its jurisdiction. In view of the importance of these interests, it seems more than likely that whatever future protection the judiciary will afford against unjustified use of government publicity to punish or defame private individuals will be of a very limited character. For the judiciary to embark upon an ambitious attempt to bar any use of government publicity in areas in which it may produce unfair coercion would be to risk hamstringing processes vital to governmental efficiency.

It is in any event questionable whether the courts ought ever to attempt so much. In a democracy the judiciary necessarily shares responsibility for protecting individual rights with the public and its legislative and executive officers, although it is characteristically American to believe that this is a responsibility that can be borne by the courts alone. It might reasonably be expected that a sense of the necessity of using restraint and fairness in applying the publicity sanction ought also to be found in other places besides the judiciary. There is, however, one unfortunate complication here present—the fact that where there is a divided responsibility, there may also be eva-

sion of responsibility. Under the American system of separation of powers, political officials have often come to expect
judges to keep their consciences for them in the area of civil
rights.

This point was argued very persuasively in the Peters case,
where the claim was made that executive officials had no desire
to administer the loyalty-security program without regard to
due process, but that they were awaiting judicial instruction
on the matter. As it was put in a brief before the Court:

> We believe that an affirmative pronouncement by this Court
> that government employees should not be compelled to risk
> their reputations and careers without due process or a fair hear-
> ing would be hailed with relief even by those who are now put-
> ting men to trial by these procedures. We do not believe that
> the men who do this enjoy their tasks. We think they would like
> to give fairer hearings. But it is politically dangerous so long as
> this procedure is followed for any government official not to
> use it. To be more fair to persons suspected of Communism than
> is necessary under the law might well be branded as softness
> towards Communism.[27]

It is of course indisputably true that, given the pressures and
anxieties that have been focused on the loyalty program in
recent times, the better part of valor as far as political officials
are concerned has been to allow the courts to drag them by
their heels into glory—in preference to any other available
mode of ascent.

Paths to Reform

The best prospects for limiting excessive coercion through
governmental use of publicity appear to lie in the direction of
procedural reform in the operation of governmental institu-

[27] *Ibid.*, p. 13.

tions that have the power to inflict punishment in this way. Such reform would have as its principal objective the reduction of unwarranted injury to the innocent wherever possible in the process of inquiry into alleged instances of unlawful behavior. In the realm of publicity, it is often very difficult for proof of innocence to catch up with an initial impression of guilt, and law enforcement by both legislative and executive agencies should show recognition of this fact in an age of instantaneous and virtually irrevocable communication of unfavorable news.

Inspiration for procedural reform can only come from a clear recognition on the part of government and the community alike of the coercive effect of adverse publicity. Standing in the way of such recognition in the past has been the fiction that governmental use of publicity does not represent constraint, since it does not inflict legal punishment upon a private person nor formally require him to do anything he does not choose to do. Wherever this fiction persists, it will be difficult to arouse sentiment or support for reform.

Within Congress, considerable attention has been given to revising the procedures of investigating committees in the interest of providing for fairer treatment of witnesses, and efforts have been made in this connection to protect witnesses against certain kinds of adverse publicity that may result from their appearance before congressional committees. In 1955, for example, the House adopted a set of procedural reforms governing the operations of its investigating committees. One of the provisions of this new legislation, which was sponsored by Representative Doyle, of California, is the requirement that a committee, if it finds that evidence may "tend to defame, degrade or incriminate any person," receive this evidence in secret session, and allow the person injured to appear as a witness and to request subpoenas of other witnesses.[28]

[28] See *Congressional Quarterly Almanac*, Vol. XI (1955), p. 382.

While the Doyle bill certainly points in the direction of reform, it was widely regarded at the time of its adoption as an ineffective effort at compromise. One critic, Representative Scott, of Pennsylvania, referred to it as "a triumph of innocuous inconsequence" and a "hasty sop to public opinion" designed "to head off effective legislation." [29] Other proposals for the reform of congressional investigating procedures have suggested much more elaborate safeguards to prevent defamation of private citizens through the investigative process. These proposals are sometimes criticized on the grounds that they provide little protection against a congressman bent on using his power in an irresponsible way. This is, of course, true, but there still remains a very compelling case for the adoption of a code of fair procedure:

> Undoubtedly no rules can guarantee the cessation of hit-and-run smears, of sensational accusations not based on evidence, of bullying inquisitors, of deliberate efforts to distort, mislead or confuse, of judgments handed down without hearing the individual condemned, of committee chairmen who ride roughshod over their fellow committee members. But the adoption of a code of procedure places stumbling blocks in the path of the demagogue and aids in evoking that public morality which in the final analysis determines what is or is not politically profitable. There is much to be said for a normative code that raises standards, educates the public to what are the fairest and hence best procedures and arms the critic with ammunition with which to attack abuse.[30]

Perhaps as important as any other reason for putting some faith in procedural reform is the fact that adherence to due process

[29] See Edward J. Heubel, "Congressional Resistance to Reform: The House Adopts a Code for Investigating Committees," *Midwest Journal of Political Science*, Vol. 1 (November, 1957), p. 327. Heubel's article is a thoroughgoing review and appraisal of congressional efforts to reform investigating procedures.

[30] Will Maslow, "Fair Procedure in Congressional Investigations: A Proposed Code," *Columbia Law Review*, Vol. 54 (June, 1954), pp. 847–48.

has always represented so strong a strand in the American constitutional tradition.

Of course any set of procedural restrictions needs to strike a balance between protecting individuals from defamation and preserving the vitality of Congress as an instrument of publicity. For as noted earlier, the legislature's preëminent functions in modern society, when so much of the initiative in matters of legislation has been seized by the executive, are the tasks of exposing the existence of abuses that need correction, and quickening the conscience of the public—engaging, in short, in the constant business of policing the work of government and educating the community.

But it is extremely important to maintain a distinction between the exposure of activities and the indictment of individuals. In the congressional inquiry into the rigging of television quiz programs, for example, the task before Congress was that of publicizing an unsavory state of affairs in an industry subject to regulation by an agency that was then under congressional scrutiny. It was not the legislature's function to pass on the guilt of every individual who had appeared as a contestant on these shows. By and large this was a distinction the committee managed to preserve (following at the same time a set of procedures that won it a commendation from the American Civil Liberties Union [31]). It did so in spite of the fact that it was under enormous temptation to concern itself with personalities rather than problems, in view of the wide public interest that existed in the television scandal and the degree to which individual contestants had been involved in fraudulent practices.

In this case as in others, the exposure of wrongdoing necessarily spotlights attention upon the behavior of particular individuals. But there is a difference between the exposure of an individual that is incidental to the investigation of a problem and an investigation that is carried on for no other purpose

[31] *New York Times,* November 6, 1959, p. 17.

than that of holding isolated individuals up to public scorn. This was the distinction the Supreme Court was reaching for in its Watkins decision when it condemned "exposure for exposure's sake." But however well intended, the Court's formulation of the case was quite inexact. "Exposure for exposure's sake," as long as it is aimed at activities rather than individuals has historically always been, and must necessarily continue to be, a proper function of congressional investigations. It only becomes improper when a legislative committee arrogates to itself a judicial function, and deliberately sets itself up to determine the guilt or innocence of particular individuals.

Needless to say, there will always be marginal cases, since crime and the criminal are not easily separated for purposes of investigation. But these cases are the exception rather than the rule. Or they would be if the penchant of American congressmen for playing the role of prosecuting attorney could be restrained. Raymond Moley once gave an explanation of this phenomenon that is worth repeating:

> . . . the county prosecutor's office provides the initial training for American political careers. It is an internship for young statesmen. And such is the force of this training that when these men reach their heart's desire as successful public figures they are in method, manner and mental bent, prosecutors still. Their psychological patterns are those of the formative years of their political apprenticeship . . . it must be recognized that eminence in the Senate of this generation has gone to a group whose contribution has been greatest in activities which were in their nature criminal prosecutions either of individual office holders or of private corporations.[32]

These lines were published in 1929, but there would be few who would deny the force of their application to American politics during the period that has since elapsed. At the same

[32] Raymond Moley, *Politics and Criminal Prosecution* (New York, 1929), pp. 236–37.

time, however, the examples of Eisenhower, Kennedy, Rockefeller, and Stevenson would suggest that a very impressive political career can be forged out of ingredients other than skill at prosecution.

Steps might also be taken to insure that defendants in law enforcement proceedings gain access to defensive publicity. It is, for example, clear that one of the most damaging aspects of the quasi judicial proceedings conducted by legislative committees is the fact that they may be quite one-sided from a publicity point of view. At an ordinary trial, a defendant may have his own character witnesses as well as an opportunity to create doubts in the public mind as to the credibility of testimony offered against him. Opportunities for such defensive publicity are often restricted at legislative hearings, while, on the other hand, the prosecution itself has the opportunity to focus and maximize the brunt of unfavorable publicity against a witness.

There are numerous ways in which this management of publicity can be carried on. For one thing, a congressional committee can schedule hearings at a time when, other news being slack, a suitable opportunity appears for catching the attention of the media of communication as well as the public. As reported by Douglass Cater, one House committee circulated a memorandum among its members which represented a "classic disquisition on the publicity requirements" for a successful investigation. Among the tactics recommended were:

1. Decide what you want the newspapers to hit hardest and then shape each hearing so that the main point becomes the vortex of the testimony. Once that vortex is reached, *adjourn*.

. . . .

5. Do not space hearings more than 24 or 48 hours apart when on a controversial subject. This gives the opposition too much opportunity to make all kinds of counter-charges and replies by issuing statements to the newspapers.

6. Don't ever be afraid to recess a hearing even for five minutes,

so that you keep the proceedings completely in control so far as creating news is concerned.[33]

In the light of tactics of this kind, it is clear that there is as much need for a sense of fair play or due process in the field of publicity as has traditionally been required in the area of law.

But it is often very difficult to restrain congressmen who are bent on publicizing derogatory information in committee files on private citizens. The chairman of the House subcommittee investigating "payola" (the practice under which record companies pay disc jockeys for playing their records) attempted to establish the principle that "during the course of investigating any problems . . . no information obtained by the subcommittee shall be made public." [34] However, this attempt to prevent premature publicity during the course of an investigation was ignored by the committee's ranking minority member, who made public evidence that Dick Clark, a television star, had played records on his show in which he had a personal financial interest. And shortly thereafter, the chairman was forced to modify his rule in order to allow members of the House access to the committee's files.

In the case of the executive as well as the legislature, self-imposed restraints can go a long way toward prevention of abuse in the power of publicity. Shortly after the Supreme Court handed down its 1959 decisions extending immunity from liability for defamation to all government officials having policy-making authority, Attorney-General Rogers sent a memorandum to the heads of each executive department and agency. In it, he cautioned government officials to use the greatest care in issuing derogatory statements in the course of their official duties. Rogers noted that while an official might not be sued for damages over a defamatory statement that was

---

[33] Douglass Cater, *The Fourth Branch of Government* (Cambridge, 1959), pp. 58–59.
[34] The Baltimore *Morning Sun,* March 12, 1960, p. 7

within the bounds of legality, he might still be subject to disciplinary action or actual removal from office by his superior. Above all, he pointed out, officials should always act "with an awareness of the vital importance of avoiding unnecessary injury to any person." [35] This kind of attitude in high places can, of course, do much to establish a climate of opinion in which subordinate officials will not find it expedient to make promiscuous use of the threat of adverse publicity in dealing with private citizens.

There are many government agencies that have gone out of their way to follow procedures which will protect private parties from unnecessary publicity. In correspondence with the Moss subcommittee investigating government information policy, for example, the Bureau of Customs defended its practice of withholding information regarding customs investigation on, among other grounds, the fact that,

> . . . the Government has a responsibility to avoid bringing the reputation of private citizens into disrepute by making public unproven allegations of wrongdoing. The very fact that Government officers are exempt from libel proceedings places an extra responsibility on them not to abuse this privilege by making public statements which they may be unable to prove in court.[36]

In this instance, however, the bureau was forced to open its records to a good deal more public inspection than it had previously allowed, since the Moss subcommittee was able to demonstrate that much of the information it was concealing involved violations of import laws which it was in the public interest to disclose.

This case points up a persistent difficulty that arises in connection with all efforts to shield private individuals from un-

---

[35] *New York Times*, July 13, 1959, p. 28.
[36] *Second Report by the Committee on Government Operations*, 85th Cong., 1st sess., House Report No. 157, February 22, 1957, p. 18.

necessary publicity. This is the fact that a strong and conflicting public interest can frequently be invoked against such secrecy by newspaper and other groups. The Office of Price
Stabilization, for example, followed the practice of withholding the names of those found guilty of ceiling-price violations, if the violations were small and were not the result of
willful design or negligence. The agency defended this policy
in its *Manual on Enforcement Information* with the statement
that "while the violator should not be permitted to keep money
he has received in excess of price ceilings, it is believed that
publicity in such instances is unfair to him." But as was pointed
out in a subsequent critique of the agency's procedure, this
policy ignored a number of other interests that were equally
well served by publicity on such matters, including the public's right to know the identity of firms that were violating the
law.[37] In any event the OPS eventually abandoned this policy
of secrecy with respect to these minor violations of its regulations.

Important as procedural reforms in the operations of government institutions can be in keeping use of the publicity
sanction within legitimate bounds,[38] there is another important direction from which a restriction in its coercive impact
can be accomplished. This is through the development of
greater intestinal fortitude in the individuals and institutions
faced with the threat or use of adverse publicity as a technique

[37] See James R. Wiggins, *Freedom or Secrecy* (New York, 1956), pp. 29–
31.

[38] This very brief treatment of procedural reform does obvious injustice to
the complexity of the subject. For a thorough and enlightening study of one
congressional committee and its procedural problems, see Robert K. Carr,
The House Committee on Un-American Activities 1945–1950 (Ithaca, 1952),
especially pp. 284–319. As Carr indicates, the problem of devising proper procedures for committee hearings also involves taking into account such other
factors as the use that may be made of publicity by certain kinds of witnesses
—e.g. Communists who take advantage of the available forum to vilify a
committee in prepared statements.

of governmental control. Against undue timidity in this regard there is no possibility of providing constitutional or legal protection. A reluctance to "stand up"—in a literal sense—for rights, that is an unwillingness on the part of private persons to acquire visibility in a controversial light, may ultimately do more to weaken limitations upon political power than the most egregious of excesses in use of the publicity sanction by government officials.

The role that the media of communication can play in curbing misuse of the power of publicity by government officials has been the subject of much discussion. One of the more startling facts revealed by the McCarthy episode in American history was the extent to which the press is helpless to prevent itself from becoming the unwitting accomplice of a government official bent on using the media of communication for the dissemination of falsehood. Although in the case of some newspapers, collaboration with the Senator was a labor of love, even those papers which were his bitterest critics seemed incapable of developing a means of covering McCarthy which would suggest the dubious veracity of much of the "news" he generated.

To be sure it is not easy to conceive of a system of control which would eliminate any possibility that the media might be forced into such involuntary collusion with a public official. The visit of Khrushchev to the United Nations General Assembly meeting in New York in 1960 brought widespread suggestions that his activities in this country should be ignored by the press, or at least given only limited coverage, since he would undoubtedly spend a great deal of time during his visit propagandizing against the United States. These suggestions were rejected by American newspapers, on the very persuasive grounds that if they engaged in this form of censorship, they would be covering the news in the same kind of political way

as the state-controlled Russian press.[39] Newspapers in a free
society have as a principal responsibility that of maintaining
an open market in the field of information to which all sources
of news have the possibility of entry. If democracy is to
survive, reliance has to be placed at some point on the good
sense of the public and its ability to sift truth from falsehood.

Before leaving the subject of governmental abuse of the
power of publicity, it should be noted that at the state level
there is one group to which the courts have given special protection against this hazard. Ever since the Supreme Court's
desegregation decision in 1954, a number of cities and states
in the South have enacted legislation designed to force local
chapters of the National Association for the Advancement of
Colored People to register and list the names of their members.
Although it has complied in part with these registration statutes, the NAACP has generally refused to furnish membership
rosters, on the grounds that such public disclosure would subject the members of a local chapter to economic harassment
and might even endanger their physical safety.[40]

After many challenges in the courts, the NAACP was upheld in its stand by the Supreme Court, which ruled in 1958
that the "inviolability of privacy in group association may in

[39] It should be noted in this connection that the opportunity for a Soviet
leader with an international reputation for duplicity to deceive the American
public is slight as compared with that which is open to a home-grown politi-
cian. The problem which plagues the news industry in the field of foreign
affairs is the fact that access to the media has become a stake in the cold war,
and an area in which the Soviets appear to have an advantage because they can
prohibit the publication of any "American" news in their journals, while a
free government has no comparable control over what appears in the press
of its own country. This unfortunately is a cross that democracy will have to
bear. Even if this country's freedom of information does represent a small
tactical asset to a totalitarian adversary, it is still the heart and soul of a democracy.

[40] In Louisiana, where NAACP affiliates did furnish the Attorney-General
with the required lists, the number of NAACP branches in the state declined
from 65 to 10, while membership dropped from 13,000 to 6,000. See *Race
Relations Law Reporter*, Vol. 5 (Summer, 1960), p. 468.

many circumstances be indispensable to preservation of freedom of association, particularly where a group espouses dissident beliefs." [41] The Court made a distinction between its ruling in this case and its position in other cases in which it had denied relief to individuals and organizations seeking to escape the necessity of making public disclosure under registration statutes. It held that in this instance the state was not able to show any substantial interest or justification for obtaining the information it requested, certainly no interest which would offset the adverse effect disclosure might have upon the right of NAACP members under the Fourteenth Amendment to "pursue their collective effort to foster beliefs which they admittedly have the right to advocate." In other cases—involving, for example, the Communist party and the Ku Klux Klan—the state has been able to demonstrate that the political organizations from which it required membership information were engaged in unlawful activities it had a right to prohibit altogether.[42] Under this ruling there is at least some kind of limited right to privacy for normal political activity (at least against state regulation), as long as the state is not able to prove an overriding need to force disclosure.

[41] *NAACP* v. *State of Alabama*, 357 U.S. 449 (1958). See also *Bates* v. *City of Little Rock*, 361 U.S. 516 (1960). Justices Black and Douglas once argued for the general application of a similar rule at the national level, in a concurring opinion to *United States* v. *Rumely*, 345 U.S. 41 (1953).

[42] In one notable case, *Bryant* v. *Zimmerman*, 278 U.S. 63 (1928), the Supreme Court upheld a New York statute aimed at forcing the Ku Klux Klan to disclose its membership in the state. For an analysis of this decision and of the general problem of disclosure laws, see Joseph B. Robison, "Protection of Associations from Compulsory Disclosure of Membership," *Columbia Law Review*, Vol. 58 (May, 1958), pp. 614–49.

CHAPTER 8

MANIPULATING PUBLIC OPINION

WHILE THE USE of exposure as a method of constraint has aroused growing concern, the most deeply rooted
of all apprehensions over the role of government publicity has
long been the fear that it will be employed to "sell" the public
on official policy. Since the beginning of this century, executive public relations activity has been attacked in Congress and
within the community as an insidious means of building up
public pressure to support the goals and programs of government agencies, or in some instances to enhance the prestige of
executive officials. There have even been occasions when legislators have feared that official propaganda might be used in
ways that would have an adverse effect upon their own election
prospects.

In 1949, for example, the Secretary of Agriculture, Charles
F. Brannan, came under bitter congressional attack because of
the informational activities carried on by the Department of
Agriculture in behalf of the ill-starred Brannan plan—a proposal to substitute a system of compensatory income payments
for the price-support program that was then the basis of agricultural policy.[1] One congressman charged that "the USDA

[1] See Reo M. Christenson, *The Brannan Plan: Farm Politics and Policy*
(Ann Arbor, 1959), pp. 114–42.

publicity machine has all stops out to win national support for
the Brannan plan." [2] Legislators were particularly incensed
when the Secretary chose the occasion of a meeting of production and marketing committeemen in St. Paul (where the ex-
penses of those in attendance had been paid for by the government) to deliver a ringing defense of the plan and a sharp attack upon those who opposed it. During this period similar
concern was voiced over the public relations activities of a
number of other agencies, including the Bureau of Reclama-
tion and the Soil Conservation Service. [3]

This legislative outcry had a long historical background. As
early as 1909, legislation was passed prohibiting the Forestry
Service from spending money to prepare articles for the benefit of outside newspapers or magazines. This was followed four
years later by the enactment of a bill of general application
to all executive agencies which provided that "no money
appropriated by this or any other act shall be used for the
compensation of any publicity expert unless specifically appropriated for that purpose." A 1919 law later prohibited administrative agencies from engaging in a wide variety of
lobbying activities that might have the effect of influencing
congressional deliberations or the passage of legislation. The
activities which were forbidden included sending telegrams
or using the mails to pressure legislators. [4]

More recently, there have been several wide-ranging legis-

[2] *Ibid.*, p. 114.
[3] See *Congressional Digest*, Vol. 30, No. 5, May, 1951, pp. 142, 144, 146,
excerpts from task force report of the Hoover Commission. The opposite
side of the coin—the great difficulty some agencies encounter in trying to
reach their clientele—are traced in Morris Janowitz, Deil Wright, and William Delany, *Public Administration and the Public—Perspectives toward
Government in a Metropolitan Community* (Ann Arbor, 1958) especially
pp. 84–100.
[4] For a description of early efforts to curb executive use of publicity, see
James L. McCamy, *Government Publicity* (Chicago, 1939), pp. 6–15; and
J. A. R. Pimlott, *Public Relations and American Democracy* (Princeton,
1951), pp. 69–101.

lative investigations into administrative publicity. In 1937 a Select Committee of the Senate, under the chairmanship of Senator Byrd, undertook such an inquiry as part of its over-all examination of the organization of executive agencies.[5] In 1947 a subcommittee of the House headed by Representative Harness carried on a similar probe in order to determine whether or not certain executive agencies had engaged in propaganda with respect to issues that were still pending before the legislature.[6] The House Select Committee on Lobbying Activities, the so-called Buchanan committee, looked into the publicity activities of executive agencies in 1950, as part of its thoroughgoing study of pressures upon the national legislature.[7]

Of the three investigatory groups, the Harness subcommittee was by far the most highly critical of the propaganda activities of administrative agencies. In its final report the subcommittee bitterly condemned "techniques of Government propaganda by which Federal officials seek to perpetuate themselves in office, generate pressures on Congress for more and bigger appropriations, and sponsor job-building enterprises in the name of national emergency or by an artificially stimulated public demand." [8] The Buchanan committee, on the other hand, argued that executive agencies have an "obligation to keep the public informed of matters within their juris-

[5] *Preliminary Report of the Select Committee to Investigate the Executive Agencies of the Government*, 75th Cong., 1st sess., Senate Report No. 1275, Aug. 16, 1937, pp. 531–53.

[6] A summary of the committee's findings may be found in the *Twenty-Third Intermediate Report of the Committee on Expenditures in the Executive Departments*, 80th Cong., 2d. sess., House Report No. 2474, Dec. 31 1948.

[7] See *General Interim Report of the House Select Committee on Lobbying Activities*, 81st Cong., 2d. sess., House Report No. 3138, Oct. 20, 1950, pp. 51–62; and *Report and Recommendations on Federal Lobbying Act*, 81st Cong., 2d. sess., House Reports No. 3239, Jan. 1, 1951, part 1, pp. 35–36; part 2, pp. 3–4.

[8] *Twenty-Third Intermediate Report of the Committee on Expenditures in the Executive Departments*, p. 2.

diction," and the committee noted that "in many cases such informational activities are conducted pursuant to specific authorization or direction of the Congress." [9]

Actually, the final reports of these committees divided very clearly along lines of partisan or ideological cleavage. The Harness subcommittee's report was a product of the period of brief Republican hegemony in the national legislature during the Eightieth Congress, and its animus was largely directed at the informational activities of agencies administering New Deal programs. Contrariwise, the Buchanan committee was dominated by Democratic congressmen who saw no reason to take offense at publicity carried on by agencies which were defending or advocating the policies of Presidents Roosevelt and Truman. In this case as in others, judgment on a set of procedures very much reflected attitudes on the policies these procedures were intended to carry out.

Of course the New Deal did make extensive use of public relations activity for partisan purposes, as other administrations before or since have tended to do. During much of its early history, the Roosevelt program came under sharp attack in wide sections of the American press, and government agencies had a strong incentive to win and maintain popular support in the face of this heavy volume of hostile criticism.[10] For some officials the fact that there existed such pronounced antagonism toward the New Deal in the private media of communication was itself justification for government public relations activity which would redress the balance.

[9] See *General Interim Report of the House Select Committee on Lobbying Activities*, p. 53.

[10] See E. Pendleton Herring, *Public Administration and the Public Interest* (N.Y., 1936), pp. 362–63, and Arthur W. MacMahon, John D. Millett and Gladys Ogden, *The Administration of Federal Work Relief* (Chicago, 1941), pp. 291–98. As these latter authors point out: "The formula of public relations for modern administration is elusive. The kind of advocacy that prejudices responsible government must be avoided. Yet administrators must be left adequately equipped to fulfill their responsibilities. Careful and continuous scrutiny by legislatures and citizens is the best guarantee that the limits of desirable administrative informational activity will be observed."

But while the accelerated pace of public information activity during the New Deal may have been caused in part by the fact that the national government was becoming increasingly involved in social and economic functions that were controversial, it is also true that many of these emerging functions represented very novel commitments on the part of government, and there was a great need for explanatory activity on the part of agencies responsible for their administration. Furthermore, since many of the newer tasks of government required that executive agencies gain the attention of great numbers of people, this explanatory activity was quick to exploit the more advanced media of communication, radio and the motion picture camera, for example. Nothing has been more remarkable about information activity today than the expansion in the size of the audience to which modern government now addresses itself.

Moreover, as the tasks of government grow in both range and complexity, this fact alone causes an inevitable increase in the scope of government information activity. And this is not a matter of bureaucratic aggrandizement alone. For the truth is that government agencies are often forced into the business of establishing information programs to meet the needs of reporters and commentators on public affairs in interpreting the wide variety of scientific and technical subjects encompassed by the work of executive agencies today. In the absence of government assistance through press releases, briefing sessions, and background conferences, the modern reporter would have a difficult if not impossible task in reporting and interpreting the work of agencies whose activities he is assigned to cover.[11]

The press officer is thus an invaluable ally to the newspaperman, even if at times he can become a serious impediment to the reporter's efforts to obtain information that an agency may

[11] See Leo C. Rosten, *The Washington Correspondents* (New York, 1937), pp. 72–77.

not wish to have disclosed, or can harass the reporter when he seeks to by-pass the press office in order to interview officials who are directly on the firing line. Not that these efforts to use the press office to choke off leaks, or to conceal internal squabbles within administration, are very successful. The brashness of American newspapermen in ferreting out information is legendary, and this, coupled with the hound-dog inquisitiveness of Congress, makes it impossible to keep very many things secret in American government today merely because they are embarrassing. But the fact that such secrets exist colors the reciprocal dependence that exists between government and the press with an attitude of mutual suspicion.

In a report published in 1950, the first Hoover Commission estimated that the publicity activities of government agencies were costing the taxpayer almost $105,000,000 annually.[12] It arrived at this figure by charging $50,000,000 a year to printing costs, $40,000,000 for mailing, and better than $13,000,000 for personal services. Figures prepared for Congress by the Bureau of the Budget and quoted in this same report showed that 45,778 persons are "now employed full time or part time on publicity or propaganda work of every kind or description." The varied tasks performed by these individuals included: "press service, radio, television, group contacts, paid advertising, traveling exhibits, motion pictures, lantern slides, traveling lecturers, photographic service, individual contacts and direct correspondence with editors and publishers. In addition, several agencies maintain separate sections to conduct programs of educational cooperation with schools, civic bodies, labor organizations and similar groups."[13] But even these efforts at itemization cannot measure the total range of governmental contact with the community in the course of day-to-

[12] The commission's report is published in the *Congressional Record* 81st Cong., 2d sess., Vol. 96, pt. 17, pp. A6861-66.
[13] *Ibid.*, p. A6861.

day operations, or fully convey how deep an impact an agency may have upon public opinion as it goes about administering the functions with which it has been charged by law.

The Control of Propaganda

The central issue to which studies of domestic information programs ordinarily address themselves is whether it is possible to enforce a meaningful distinction between proper and improper activity by executive agencies in the field of publicity. Even the Harness subcommittee was forced to temper its highly critical comments on government publicity with the acknowledgement that "there is a fine line between legitimate information service, and activity on the part of agencies and individuals which is designed to condition the public mind, and . . . it will take legislation drawn with meticulous care to prevent improper action without infringing on legitimate services." [14]

Of course there are those who question the wisdom of any government involvement in information activity. The task force report of the first Hoover Commission took such a skeptical stand in reviewing the informational program of the Bureau of Mines:

All programs of education by the Government tend eventually to reflect official thought, official opinion and official aims. In these circumstances, the function of education inevitably is diluted by the pressures of politics and propaganda. The best safeguard possible for the whole process of education is to keep it in the hands of the people themselves, through their own cooperative organizations, and to remove it as far as possible from direction, guidance, and influence by the administrative officials

[14] *Twenty-Third Intermediate Report of the Committee on Expenditures in the Executive Departments*, p. 9.

of the Government. All the history of national thought-control agencies in other lands supports this conclusion.[15]

Over the years Congress has used a variety of techniques in an effort to curb what it regards as improper activity on the part of executive agencies in the field of publicity, including prohibitions upon the employment of publicity experts, legislation forbidding certain government agencies from sending information through the mail except in response to specific requests from the public, and restrictions upon the use of appropriated funds for public relations activity. None of these barriers to executive publicity has been altogether effective, as is evident from the fact that it has proven necessary to reenact such restrictions so frequently over the past half-century, and no one has ever been prosecuted for violating any of these statutes. The ban on the employment of publicity experts, for example, has been commonly evaded by giving these employees somewhat different titles, including information specialist, director of public relations, and chief educational officer.[16]

The basic difficulty which confronts all attempts to prevent improper publicity is that few if any executive agencies could discharge their governmental responsibilities at all if they were obliged to work under very severe restrictions on the amount of informational activity they could carry on. For some agencies, the informational function is in fact their very reason for existence. The Office of Education, the Children's Bureau, the Extension Service—agencies such as these have historically had no more central purpose than that of disseminating information and educating the public on such matters as school organization, child labor, and improved methods of farming. For other agencies publicity may play a less stra-

[15] As quoted in the *Congressional Record*, 81st Cong., 2d sess., Vol. 96, pt 17, p. A6862.
[16] See McCamy, *op. cit.*, p. 7.

tegic role, but its significance is nonetheless very great.[17] As noted already, agencies with regulatory responsibility have found publicity an indispensable instrument for arousing public knowledge and support of their goals.

Moreover, under the Administrative Procedure Act and other legislation, a great many agencies are now compelled by law to disseminate information about themselves and their internal organization and procedures. Failure to do so might bring them under legal or political attack for concealing information from the public. Congress itself has introduced innumerable reporting requirements in an effort to insure that executive agencies keep it adequately informed. As previous chapters have shown, its principal complaints in this area have more often that not been against the efforts of executive officials to conceal rather than to publicize information lodged within their jurisdiction.[18] And Congressmen frequently call upon executive agencies for assistance and information in preparing speeches or for advice on pending legislation.

Certain kinds of public relations activity on the part of administrative agencies arouse almost universal objection. One is the use of publicity for the exclusive purpose of promoting the career and status (or perhaps the political aspirations) of an executive official, rather than the statutory objectives for which the agency was created. In 1958, the House Subcommittee on Government Information severely criticized a press release from the Department of Commerce entitled "Biography and Human Interest Features on Sinclair Weeks, United States Secretary of Commerce." The subcommittee described the press release as a "prime example of the use of public funds for the personal glorification of a Federal official," noting that "Congress did not appropriate money for the Department of Commerce to spend in describing how Secretary Weeks' in-

[17] See Pimlott, *op. cit.*, pp. 76–80.
[18] See especially Chap. 3.

terest in baseball 'rises to fever pitch,' " during the summer, or
" 'how decked out in a chef's hat and apron, he prepares and
serves griddle cakes for his guests to cover with Cat Bow
maple sirup ' " [19]

Another member of Eisenhower's Cabinet, Secretary of
Labor James P. Mitchell, was similarly embarrassed when the
department issued reprints of an article suggesting the Secretary as Vice-President Nixon's running mate in the 1960
presidential election. This was during the period when Mitchell
was being widely discussed as a possibility for the vice-presi-
dential slot on the Republican ticket, and the Secretary had
given some indication of his availability for the nomination.
The release was withdrawn on the same day on which it was
issued, after several correspondents to whom it had been
directed raised questions as to the propriety of an official communication of this kind.

To be sure, any publicity which tends to enhance the public
stature of an administrative agency inevitably reflects credit
upon its chief executive. It is, therefore, impossible to prevent
executive officials from deriving some benefit from the work
of their agencies, whether or not they engage in any deliberate
or overt attempt at self-aggrandizement. The public reputation that has been achieved by J. Edgar Hoover in recent
decades has been a source of considerable irritation in some
quarters. In 1940 Senator George Norris referred to the head
of the FBI as "the greatest hound for publicity on the American continent today." [20] And yet the plain fact of the matter
is that, whatever efforts Hoover may have made in his own behalf, his stature in the public eye derives primarily from the
achievements of the FBI and the respect with which it is held
by the general public. The notion that "good administration

---

[19] *Thirty-Fifth Report by the Committee on Government Operations,*
85th Cong., 2d sess., House Report No. 2578, Aug. 13, 1958, p. 219.
[20] Don Whitehead, *The FBI Story* (New York, 1956), p. 177

is good politics" has as an obvious corollary the fact that the best publicity is a popular administrative record. Of course, administrative accomplishments may well be exaggerated, and they can easily be distorted, but in an open society it is still very difficult to make a silk purse out of a sow's ear through propaganda alone.

There also exists widespread agreement that administrative agencies ought not to engage in publishing material that is of a merely trivial nature. In 1960 heavy congressional fire was directed at an on-the-job training manual that the Air Force had issued which instructed enlisted men on how to wash an officer's dog, make his bed, and mix his drinks.[21] This manual was withdrawn following protests from Representative Frank Kowalski, of Connecticut. Another manual that also came under censure at this time gave extensive information on the handling of officers' parties, supplying enlisted men with helpful hints on such matters as the correct technique of getting customers to order alcoholic rather than non-alcoholic beverages on bingo nights.[22] In cases of this kind, where government informational activity verges on the ludicrous, pressure for economy lends additional strength to the normal congressional distaste for public relations programs.

An effort has also been made to establish the principle that executive publicity ought to be entirely objective in character. Insofar as this proposition suggests that executive agencies ought to be truthful in their communications to Congress and the public, it would not provoke serious dissent, except perhaps in cases like the U-2 affair, where, as noted earlier, falsehood has been justified in the interests of national security.

[21] *New York Times*, Feb. 4, 1960, p. 1.
[22] *New York Times*, Feb. 19, 1960, p. 1. One other Air Force manual that came under attack at this time, contained a statement that greatly incensed congressmen: "Another rather silly remark often heard concerning security is that Americans have a right to know what is going on. Most people realize the foolhardiness of such a suggestion."

But there is always room for disagreement as to whether any particular piece of informational material actually is as objective as it might be.

The fact that one man's truth may indeed be another's falsehood was pointed up in 1956 when the House Subcommittee on Government Information complained that the Rural Electrification Administration had deleted a chart from its 1953 report showing the cost to REA borrowers of power procured from private utility companies as compared with that obtained from public power agencies.[23] Instead the REA had published a chart showing the average cost of power derived from both sources, thus eliminating an apparent indication of the cheaper cost of public power. At the same time, however, the agency continued to furnish data on comparative costs to "those persons requesting it."

In urging the REA to restore the original chart, the House subcommittee argued that if the agency failed to do so, it "might lead to the conclusion that the chart has been deleted because it reflected unfavorable comparisons." The subcommittee at this time advanced the theory that a government agency has an obligation not only to make information available but to do so in ways that will leave no room for misunderstanding by the general public:

> It is well to say that the basic data are available "upon request." But few people or organizations have the staff and adding machines to work out statistical comparisons as REA has done prior to 1953.

> Facts about the operation of government can be obscured at times by deluging the public with too many detailed statistics. It is the obligation of Government to summarize these statistics with clarity so that they can be understood by the average citizen.

[23] See *Second Report by the Committee on Government Operations*, 85th Cong., 1st sess., House Report No. 157, Feb. 22, 1957, pp. 53–60.

. . . Government agencies have a duty not only to make information available to the public but also to provide the facts of Government in a usable, understandable form.[24]

Eventually the REA was forced to retreat and resume publishing the chart on relative costs of private and public power, even though the agency contended that the graph was misleading because it ignored geographical and other factors which have a significant effect upon the variation in cost.

A sensible distinction can also be drawn between those officials for whom public relations is a perfectly proper kind of activity and those for whom it is not, a distinction which rests essentially on the notion that politically appointed policy-making officials have the right to engage in publicity whether or not it smacks of partisan advocacy, but that this same privilege is not enjoyed by career civil servants, whose tenure and status rest on the assumption that they will remain politically neutral. The difficulty with this distinction is that it can only be maintained when it is supported by conventions that are not present in the American political system, including agreement that a cabinet member bears full responsibility for all policy articulated in the executive department under his jurisdiction.

In this country, however, Congress does not accept such "rules of the game." When the heads of executive departments become vigorous advocates of controversial policies, they may be subject to sharp attack on the grounds that they are using their office to engage in unseemly propaganda. During President Truman's administration the Federal Security Administrator, Oscar Ewing, and, as already noted, Charles F. Brannan, the Secretary of Agriculture, were bitterly criticized for speeches and other informational activity aimed at winning public support for new medical care and agricultural programs.[25] Underlying this criticism was the apparent assump-

---

[24] *Ibid.,* p. 59.
[25] See *Congressional Digest,* Vol. 30, no. 5, May, 1951.

tion that a cabinet member should confine himself to the strictly routine chores of administration, and that it is somehow improper for such an official to advocate or defend policy recommendations.

The convention of cabinet responsibility is also disregarded from another direction—the tendency of career administrators to be drawn into the vortex of policy dispute. Ever since the end of World War II, there has been recurrent controversy over participation by career military officers in public debate over defense policy. Republicans were highly critical of this practice during the Truman administration. In 1947 the Harness committee issued a strong indictment of the activities of the War Department in promoting universal military training through speeches and public appearances by army officers and civilian employees.[26] Later, in 1950, there was similar Republican objection to the alignment of the joint chiefs of staff on the administration's side of the Truman-MacArthur controversy.

Since 1952, on the other hand, the Democrats have also had occasion to question the role of the military in political combat. In January of 1960, for example, Senator Hubert Humphrey charged that recent political activity by Defense Department officials was "unethical and beneath the dignity of the Administration." These officials had participated in fundraising dinners carried on across the country, so-called "dinners with Ike." President Eisenhower subsequently defended his Defense Department subordinates on, among other grounds, the fact that they were "politically appointed."

However, writing in the *New York Times*, columnist Arthur Krock later argued that all high officials in both the State and the Defense Departments should rigorously abstain from

---

[20] *Fourth Intermediate Report of the Committee on Expenditures in the Executive Departments*, 80th Cong., 1st sess., House Report No. 1073, July 24, 1947.

political combat, since the programs within their jurisdiction demand bipartisan support.[27] This adds a dimension of complexity to the relationship between politics and administration in American government. Some officials who are actually political appointees are nevertheless expected to refrain from political activity, if the programs they administer are considered to be "above politics."

In spite of the fact that none of these efforts to develop a formula for singling out improper executive publicity has been altogether successful, whether pursued through statutory or extra-legal channels, it should not be assumed that this campaign has been altogether without meaningful effect. The mere existence of public concern over this problem has been an important deterrent against any incipient tendency toward government brain-washing. Even if there exists no real anticipation that executive officials who carry on propaganda will actually be prosecuted, there is still the ever-present possibility of an unpleasant investigation, a reduction in appropriations, or the harassment of personnel who engage in such practices, and these "hidden persuaders" represent perhaps the most important barrier against improper activity in the field of publicity as far as executive agencies are concerned.

Managing the News

Concern over the influence of government upon public opinion has largely focused on the possibility that executive officials might force-feed the communications media with information designed to win public support for official points of view. Actually, however, the real strength of government in the communications process comes from an entirely different source—its ability to trade on the hunger of the communi-

[27] See *New York Times,* Jan. 29, 1960, p. 24.

cations media for news about public affairs—a hunger that only government can, in many areas, gratify. Critics of government information activity often draw a picture of newsmen as the unwilling victims of government propaganda. Often, however, newspapers themselves are so anxious to get the "inside story" from official sources on a current issue of domestic or international importance that they become willing if not enthusiastic collaborators in the process by which government influences public opinion.[28]

Of fundamental importance here is the fact that public officials have the capacity to initiate news about public affairs, and the press and other media of communication are eager customers for material of this kind, since it is grist for their own mills. Thus, when in the midst of a domestic controversy over the adequacy of our system of national defense, President Eisenhower made a sudden flight to Cape Canaveral, this trip, which was widely dramatized by press, radio, and television, was worth tons of informational material designed to show that the administration was giving attentive care to the needs of national defense. In this case as in others, it was not propaganda alone, but an executive act which proved an effective stroke in the field of public opinion—and it was an act to which the media of communication were happy to give prominent coverage because of its news value. This was favorable publicity of a kind that no amount of informational activity could have procured.

Sometimes, in an effort to heighten public interest in current affairs, the media may even serve the purposes of government officials by investing these events with a great deal more drama than they would seem objectively to exhibit. This is

[28] By far the most penetrating study of the entire range of relationships among government, the press, and public opinion, is Douglass Cater, *The Fourth Branch of Government* (New York, 1959). See also Leo Rosten, *op. cit.*, and James E. Pollard, *The Presidents and the Press* (New York, 1947). Cabell Phillips, *et al.*, *Dateline: Washington* (New York, 1949).

certainly the case with national party conventions, about the dullness of which there are frequent complaints from the public. At the time of both national conventions in 1960, but particularly in the case of the Republican meeting in Chicago, television commentators labored manfully to adorn these proceedings with every bit of contest and color imaginable, even when the outcome of important business seemed cut and dried and entirely predictable. The television networks, which had gone to considerable expense and trouble to provide minute by minute coverage of these national conventions, had an enormous investment at stake in their efforts to gain and hold the attention of the national audience, and in the end the major political parties owed the communications industry a debt of gratitude for its efforts to arouse and maintain public interest in their proceedings. The "election industry" in this country has come to have as much an interest in the entertainment value of political events as the politicians themselves.

The dependence of the media of communications upon government and official sources for news finds no better illustration than the prominent place newspapers are now willing to give to background briefings, off-the-record conferences, and stories handed out under the authority of "high-ranking" or "usually reliable" sources—the whole range of phenomena comprehended by the phrase "government leak." [29] Reliance upon official assistance of this kind is particularly pronounced in the field of foreign affairs, where behind-the-scenes interviews and other means of communication enable newspapers to apprise themselves of the meaning of events and thus make sense out of them for their readers. Douglass Cater has noted that it is the absence of this kind of official assistance which makes accurate reporting so difficult a task in the Soviet Union.[30]

[29] See Rosten, *op. cit.*, pp. 98–103; and Cater, *op. cit.*, pp. 128–141.
[30] Cater, *op. cit.*, p. 179.

But even while serving their own interests, newspapermen nonetheless make a large contribution to the purposes
of government officials by the way in which they dutifully
report material that comes to them via so-called "leaks." For
the leak has long had a great deal of functional utility within
government. One very important purpose which it serves is
that of allowing public officials to launch trial balloons which
will test public sentiment on policy proposals or projected appointments that are still in the stage of preliminary exploration. Used in this way, the leak can be a major asset in a system
of government by public opinion, since it enables executive
officials to avoid premature commitment to policies whose un-
popularity will make them unworkable, or it allows administrators to discern where an educational campaign is necessary in order to correct popular misunderstandings.

While the leak serves as a means of creating policy, it can
also be employed as a technique for its destruction, insofar as
executive officials do use the leak as a weapon for waging un-
derground war upon one another. An official who loses out
in a struggle over policy, appropriations, or jurisdiction within
the inner councils of the executive, may well carry his cause
into the arena of publicity. By means of off-the-record conferences with reporters, he can convey his own adverse judgments on policies that have just been decided upon, in the hope
that public opinion may be aroused in time to force the administration to reverse its judgment. Used in this way, the leak
flouts presidential directives which require a front of executive
unanimity once decisions have been reached. But it provides
reporters (and eventually the public) with an intimate view
of executive deliberations and differences of opinion that
would not otherwise be known, and may thus enhance the influence of public opinion upon executive decisions. Of course,
the negative effect of such leaks should not be minimized,
especially where, in the area of foreign affairs, they serve to
embarrass this country in its relations with other nations.

Sometimes the leak may be employed in an even more devi-
ous way. A public official may use it to get himself on record
in opposition to policies that he feels to be unpopular, even
though he himself is, by virtue of his position, constrained to
render them ostensible support. Vice-President Nixon used
this tactic very extensively in the period preceding the Republican convention in 1960. Speaking often through press aides,
he let it be known that there were many points on which he
differed from President Eisenhower—e.g., on federal aid to
education—but that it would be inappropriate for him to take
issue publicly with his chief executive. Needless to say, this
course of action has much to recommend it as a political tactic.
It creates doubt as to where an official does actually stand on
a controversial issue and thus allows him to draw simultaneous
support from groups with conflicting points of view. Eventually, if public support does swing decisively in one direction, he may be able to claim that this indeed was his view all
along.

In order to understand the influence that government exerts
over public opinion, it is thus necessary to be aware not only
of the techniques available to public officials for exerting such
control, but also of certain basic considerations that make the
media susceptible to being used in this way. In the field of information activity, the relationship between government and
the press is one of mutual advantage. To be sure there is
abundant opportunity for government to manipulate the press
by, for example, timing releases in order to catch the maximum
audience and on occasion by saturating the news columns with
items favorable to itself when it wishes to distract public attention from events or disclosures that do it no credit. In the
end, government officials may have a great deal to say about
the shape of the news.

But—and this must also be recognized—the press also manip-
ulates the government and it, too, plays a large role in affecting
the contours of the news. It is clear, for example, that pressure

from the communications media can easily push government officials into premature publicity. This may have been a prime source of trouble in the U-2 affair, where the fact that government officials initially issued false statements on the incident may be traced in part to the consideration that they were under strong pressure from the media of communication for a speedy official explanation of what had occurred. Where discreet silence is called for as official policy, it may be very difficult to maintain such reserve in the face of insistent demands for information from newspaper reporters.

Publicity and Public Debate

In the light of world events over the last several decades, it is not surprising that fears should so often be expressed over the possibility that the national government might someday acquire the capacity to brain-wash the population into docile and complete acceptance of official policies through propaganda alone. Experience abroad, particularly the case of Nazi Germany and the Communist regimes in both Europe and Asia, as well as Nasser in Egypt and Castro in Cuba, suggest the powerful role that propaganda may play in winning and shoring up popular support for a dictator. The Ministry of Truth, as Orwell ironically named it in his novel *1984*, is second only to the ministry of police in the apparatus of modern dictatorship, and with the passage of time, and the pacification of rebellious elements, propaganda may even come to supplant coercion at the center of modern systems of authoritarian control.

And yet, it is extremely risky to base calculations about the future of democracy upon the experience of totalitarian societies. The structure of power within a free society is so altogether different from that which prevails in a dictatorship that comparisons are certain to be misleading. The essence of a liberal society, one of the conditions upon which freedom depends in any community, is the existence of social forces which make it possible to mobilize effective opposition against the power of the state. The presence of this countervailing power means that public opinion can be aroused against the government as well as in its behalf. In the pluralist environment that is the essence of democracy, government never monopolizes all the instruments of persuasion, and under the American system of separation of powers, it is even possible to find the opposition entrenched within the structure of government itself.

Thus, in 1947, when executive agencies under Democratic control were suspected of having used propaganda to win public support for such causes as public housing and socialized medicine, Republicans in Congress were able to launch an investigation which not only exposed these alleged efforts at brain-washing but also made a very strong case before the bar of public opinion against these very same New Deal programs. As a matter of fact, one of the minority members of the Harness subcommittee wrote a dissenting opinion in which he criticized the report submitted by his colleagues on the grounds that "it is designed to accomplish the same purposes for which the subcommittee has criticized the Federal agencies. . . . I consider that the report is slanted, partisan, and at least partially propaganda." [31]

It is essential, therefore, to guard against accepting extreme claims for the power of internal propaganda in a democracy. In a society such as ours, which tends to make a fetish of the art of persuasion (witness the overriding importance assigned to such processes as education, advertising, and salesmanship) the importance of public relations activity may easily be ex-

[31] See *Twenty-Third Intermediate Report of the Committee on Expenditures in the Executive Departments*, p. 11.

aggerated. It has become fashionable to claim that Madison Avenue advertising techniques have greatly altered American politics in recent years. If this is true, it is difficult to see where this is any more than a change in political technology—a variation in the style but not in the substance of politics. Television and radio may give politicians more effective vehicles for carrying on election campaigns, but they certainly do not give altogether new directions to political life. They do not, for example, change the nature of the issues about which politicians dispute, or the character of the appeals with which they seek to win votes.

Moreover, the influence of modern techniques of communication in building up candidates is often overemphasized. Sometimes these techniques are important, but on other occasions they may be merely superfluous. President Eisenhower, for example, was a hero of immeasurable proportions to the American people long before the barrage of publicity surrounding his candidacy in 1952 and 1956, and it is difficult to believe that the frenetic use of advertising techniques in his behalf added one cubit to his already towering stature in the eyes of the American people.[32] Some part of this tendency to exaggerate the importance of publicity may be traced to the fact that advertising and public relations agencies are themselves so eager to claim credit for achievements for which they may not be entirely responsible.[33]

When this much has been said, however, the potential impact of government propaganda cannot be discounted even in a democracy. One area in which its influence may assume strategic importance is the field of foreign affairs.[34] Here a number of

[32] For an analysis and somewhat different point of view on the public relations activities carried on in behalf of Eisenhower, see Stanley Kelley, Jr., *Professional Public Relations and Political Power* (Baltimore, 1956), Chaps. 5 and 6.

[33] This tendency is visible at many points in the study by Vance Packard, *The Hidden Persuaders* (New York, 1957).

[34] And of course in the field of international propaganda, with which

factors conspire to give the voice of government a special weight in the process by which the public forms its opinions. For one thing national pride and self-interest tend to blunt the sharp edge of debate in the field of foreign policy, since dissent always runs the risk of being labeled as treason. Moreover, in this area there are fewer independent sources of information upon which critics can draw in order to refute official government doctrine than is the case elsewhere. And it must be remembered that foreign affairs may not clearly impinge on the voter's awareness of his own self-interest, and there is a greater tendency to take the government's word for it on matters so remote from the average person's experience.

In other areas of policy, where these considerations do not operate, the influence of government is correspondingly reduced. In such fields as agriculture, labor, business, conservation—across the whole range of domestic affairs—there are pressure groups which have a vested interest in seeing that governmental efforts at persuasion are subject to constant scrutiny. Where necessary, this official propaganda may be matched and counter-balanced by broadsides from one of these private groups. By way of pointing up the comparison, it may be said that while in the field of foreign affairs the influence of government propaganda bears some resemblance to that of the monopolist in a market economy, its position in other areas is a great deal more like that of a seller competing on relatively even footing with salesmen for other points of view.

Of course, this competition is never "perfect"—executive agencies do have distinctive characteristics as instruments of persuasion. They suffer from certain disadvantages—as, for example, the fact that agencies like the Department of Labor are

---

this book does not deal, government communications have played a strategic role in modern times. See Murray Dyer, *The Weapon on the Wall* (Baltimore, 1959). This role may be especially important in Asia and Africa, where native means of communication are relatively undeveloped.

regarded as speaking primarily for special groups, and their influence with the rest of the community is correspondingly reduced. And executive agencies have certain assets, not the least of which is the fact that their statements come from an official source and thus may have a credibility they would not otherwise possess. In its inquiry into executive propaganda, the Harness subcommittee put particular stress upon the advantage this official status gives to governmental communications:

> The average citizen . . . assumes his Federal Government to be objective, impartial, and fair in its information services. He ordinarily accepts as authoritative that information which comes from Government through official channels. Whereas the individual might reject propaganda coming to him from other sources, he is more likely to be receptive to it when it is offered in the guise of "information" which comes through official channels.[35]

While this statement exaggerates the aura of truthfulness which surrounds official statements, it is important in another way. It suggests a standard of veracity to which all executive agencies can well repair. (So too, for that matter, could congressional committees.) For if the utility of government by discussion is to be preserved, then that discussion should be informed, wherever possible, by governmental communications that attain the highest standards of truthfulness—a standard that rules out sophisticated as well as simple-minded attempts at deceit. When the Atomic Energy Commission, for example, justifies continued testing of nuclear weapons on the grounds that such testing is necessary for the development of a so-called "clean bomb"—this use of slogans may well have the effect of misleading public discussion on a critical issue of national policy.

But it will never be possible, or wise, to deny executive agen-

---

[35] See *Twenty-Third Intermediate Report of the Committee on Expenditures in the Executive Departments*, p. 7.

cies the right of entry into the forum of public debate. Congress sometimes gives indication that it would like to do this, an attitude which seems based on legislative jealousy of efforts by all other institutions to influence public opinion except itself.[36] But while the legislature has a pre-eminent role it by no means has an exclusive one to play in the process of public discussion. As long as executive agencies have policy responsibilities, they will inevitably be expected to furnish information and advocate change in areas under their jurisdiction. Moreover, given the fact that executive officials are among the chief sources of expertise in many areas, their contribution to public debate can go a long way to raise the tone of this discussion. In the end it may be information from the executive which, more than any other factor, insures the rationality of final decision.

In any final appraisal of the ability of government to sell official policy, the one fact which stands out above all others is the extent to which executive agencies are able to mold public attitudes not through the release of information alone—the "propaganda" against which critics have traditionally inveighed—but through their ability to make news, by holding conferences, conducting studies, submitting legislative proposals, and in a host of other ways. This is a power that the democratic process may well be able to contain in the field of domestic policy, where there are many powerful private groups which can monitor official pronouncements and offset any misleading effect they might have with criticisms which the public will respect. But, as has already been pointed out, there is real reason for concern as to whether this system of countervailing power operates with anything like the same effectiveness in the field of foreign policy and national defense—areas where official doctrine carries impressive weight and where official error may bring awesome catastrophe.

[36] See Zechariah Chafee, Jr., *Government and Mass Communications* (Chicago, 1947), Vol. II, p. 765.

CHAPTER 9

PUBLICITY, SECRECY AND DEMOCRACY

IN THE YEARS that have elapsed since Congress first debated the wisdom of giving the president extensive control over the establishment of post roads, there has been a dramatic expansion in the scale of government information activity. In large part this expansion has reflected changes in the technology of mass communications, for it is now possible for public officials to enter into direct and immediate contact with a vast segment of the nation's population. But other factors have been at work as well, including the lengthening shadow now cast by foreign affairs and national defense—areas of public policy where the state has traditionally exercised the power to release or withhold information at its own discretion, and where the scope of information subject to such control has grown enormously with the alliance between science and the military that has sprung up since World War II.

Certainly, there is no more striking development in recent American politics than the ascendancy of publicity in all phases of the governmental process. In the struggle for power that is at the center of our political system—the contest between president and Congress—the traditional ability of the chief executive to center attention upon himself as head of state has been increasingly challenged by congressional efforts to manipulate the investigative power so as to gain a proportionate share of the nation's headlines. Publicity has also come to the fore as an important new weapon in the quest for power within both the legislative and executives branches of government, providing politicians with a new technique for moving up in our political hierarchy. In the hands of administrative officials, publicity is the main avenue through which the public is acquainted (even more than it may desire) with the objectives and achievements of executive agencies. And finally, while their effectiveness may often be exaggerated, public relations techniques have come to assume an expanding role in American election campaigns.

A great deal of attention has been devoted in these pages to the impact of publicity as a technique of law enforcement. In this area the power of publicity threatens to undermine the "rule of law" that has long been a fundamental postulate of the American constitutional system—the notion that the exercise of governmental power can be contained within fixed legal limits. For there is no doubt that the ability of government to control through publicity opens up a channel through which official power may easily flow beyond the boundaries of fixed legal categories. What a government official is not authorized to accomplish through legal prosecution, he may now be able to achieve through the threat of adverse publicity. It is this fact that has aroused growing concern about the use of publicity as a law enforcement device by both legislative and executive officials, when otherwise it might be viewed as simply another innovation in the ancient process of curbing violations of community norms.

And the fact that publicity does have widespread utility as an instrument of law enforcement has already been demonstrated. It has been put to varied use in such areas as food and drug regulation, the improvement of job opportunities for minority groups, and the control of subversive political activity. It is, however, this very effectiveness of the publicity sanction which has presented executive agencies, the legislature and the courts with the challenge to develop ethical and legal restraints that will prevent publicity from being used to inflict unwarranted damage upon private persons while it is serving legitimate purposes as an instrument of social control.

The nature of this challenge is pointed up in the regulation of subversive activity. Used indiscriminately, there is no doubt that the publicity sanction can easily constrict the opportunity for diversity, risks, and even mistakes in lawful political beliefs and associations. At the extreme, it may seriously threaten the political free enterprise which is certainly as important to a democratic community as the additional margin of safety that may accrue from public control of subversive movements. The episode of McCarthyism in recent American politics, where the threat of adverse publicity was widely employed to intimidate political opposition and to stifle public debate, suggests the danger of irresponsible use of the power of publicity in controlling alleged subversive activity.

And yet, the fact of the matter is that publicity is an extremely effective instrument for combatting subversive activities in a democracy, since these movements must be carried on secretly in the face of a hostile public opinion, and exposure alone is often sufficient to drive them out of existence. It was in fact one of the chief recommendations of President Truman's Committee on Civil Rights, a group whose report represented a milestone in the protection of democratic liberties in this country,[1] that public exposure be used as a primary weapon against the activities of both Fascist and Communist political movements. Among the other advantages which publicity has

[1] See *To Secure These Rights*, Report of the President's Committee on Civil Rights (Washington, 1947), p. 164.

over formal legal restraints as a method of control is the fact that it operates immediately, rather than waiting for the cumbersome processes of litigation to be completed. (The Subversive Activities Control Board has been trying for over eight years to complete the legal steps necessary to require the Communist party in the United States to register as a subversive organization.)

Democracy and Dictatorship

It is interesting to note that use of the publicity sanction is by no means restricted to democratic societies. In Soviet law enforcement, which may fairly be said never to miss a trick as far as sanctions are concerned, the defendant may be confronted not only with the formidable array of penalties provided for in the Soviet legal system, as for example imprisonment at forced labor, but also with the necessity of making a public confession so as to heap upon his own head the full weight of public obloquy. This practice may be said to be a refinement in cruelty in using the publicity sanction: the defendant is forced to call it upon himself. But poignant evidence of its effectiveness in Soviet society is to be found in Nikolai Bukharin's confession before the Supreme Court of the U.S.S.R. where, in acknowledging the justice of his own impending execution, he states:

> . . . when you ask yourself: "Very well, suppose you do not die; suppose by some miracle you remain alive, again what for? Isolated from everybody, an enemy of the people, in an inhuman position, completely isolated from everything that constitutes the essence of life." [2]

[2] See Thomas C. Mendenhall, Basil D. Henning, and Archibald S. Foord, *The Dynamic Force of Liberty in Modern Europe* (New York, 1952), p. 124. Bukharin's special problem was his need to reconcile himself with a political party which he accepted as the authentic voice of public opinion.

Devout Communist that he was, Bukharin was here seeking expiation before the Marxist idol of history as well as before the bar of public opinion in his confession. It is in democratic societies that the impact of public disgrace falls with greatest weight as a sanction in law enforcement. This is because public opinion tends to become the only arbiter of value in democratic societies, and to be condemned by public opinion is to be condemned by the highest court in the land.

Three of the principal commentators on American democracy, De Tocqueville, Bryce, and more recently David Riesman, have given eloquent testimony to the force that public opinion thus exerts in American democracy. For De Tocqueville, public favor in a democracy "seems as necessary as the air we breathe, and to live at variance with the multitude is, as it were, not to live." [3] In Bryce's view the sovereignty of public opinion in American society is no less total: "He whom the multitude condemns . . . has no further court of appeal to look to. Rome has spoken. His cause has been heard and judgment has gone against him." [4] Finally, Riesman, in his analysis of contemporary American society writes: "Approval itself, irrespective of content, becomes almost the only unequivocal good. . . . One makes good when one is approved of. Thus all power not merely some power is in the hands of the actual or imaginary approving group." [5]

The use of publicity in law enforcement is but one illustration of the parallels that have emerged between dictatorship and democracy with respect to the role of public opinion in the operations of the contemporary state. In the light of these similarities, it is possible to suggest that we stand today on the brink of a new era in which the differences among political sys-

[3] Alexis De Tocqueville, *Democracy in America*, edited by Phillips Bradley (New York, 1945), Vol. II, p. 261.
[4] James Bryce, *The American Commonwealth* (New York, 1911), Vol. II, p. 353.
[5] David Riesman, *The Lonely Crowd* (New Haven, 1950), p. 49.

tems will become increasingly less distinct, as all governments come to depend upon the sustaining force of public opinion for authority and legitimacy. Dictatorships may, in the course of time, find it possible to put much less reliance upon the apparatus of terror and coercion upon which authoritarian government has traditionally been based. Instead, the system of totalitarian control will come to rest on the conditioning of public opinion to accept the aims of official policy and, with the withering away of opposition, the emergence of subjects who shun political deviation as much as they would any other abnormality which denies them the respect of the community. Like Bukharin, the average Soviet citizen may eventually be a person who finds it intolerable to endure the lonely isolation of dissent and the stigma of political heresy.

From this perspective, it can be predicted that democracies will also undergo an evolutionary process which, while tracing a different course, will eventually arrive at the same destination. Without in any way abridging the constitutional restraints through which the powers of democratic government have always been limited, free societies may nonetheless move toward a pattern of political conformity through the force of public opinion alone. Political dissent may become every bit as hazardous in a democratic as in a totalitarian community, when the stigma of alienation from the community becomes sufficient to deter all but the most hardy of individuals from following the course that their own conscience dictates.

If political systems were to converge in this fashion, it would require very little alteration in the visible forms of democratic and totalitarian government. In constitutional societies the entire framework of legal freedoms could remain intact, representing a set of ideals that would be as often proclaimed as they were assiduously neglected. Opposing parties might still continue to function, but the range of issues over which debate takes place would narrow over the years. Increasingly, elections would turn on the personalities and the administrative capacities of candidates rather than on any set of ideological differences by which parties were divided. The aim and highest ideal of this kind of democracy would be the avoidance of conflict. Consensus would be enthroned as the first principle of political life.

It could hardly be expected that dictatorships would abolish the entire apparatus of control used for enforcing consent. Needless to say, there would be powerful bureaucratic forces within the police system which would resist any such drastic change. Nevertheless, coercion would gradually play a less and less important role in the everyday operations of the state, as the proportion of the population which needed to be controlled by the methods of violence slowly shrank. Eventually, it might be possible to permit all subjects the same formal freedoms that are allowed in Western democracies, as long as the state could reasonably expect that social pressure would be sufficient to prevent these freedoms from being used to advocate radical change.

Of course this is a nightmarish conception of the worst of all possible worlds. Developments which might lead to this outcome are certainly visible on the contemporary scene, and an effort has been made in these pages to indicate something of their character and importance. But in neither dictatorial nor democratic communities is the sovereignty of public opinion as yet even close to the point where it is possible for despots to dispense with coercion, or for democrats to despair of the possibility of freely expressing dissent in the face of unfavorable public sentiment. What is important and still true, however, is the fact that the power of public opinion does provide a means by which the difference between a free and a totalitarian community can be progressively narrowed, as the free society becomes gradually less free and the dictatorial system in turn has an opportunity to become less overtly coercive.

In the area of foreign policy, it might be noted, there is little question but that American democracy has moved very close to the point of consensus today. With respect to virtually all major issues of the cold war, the broad outlines of policy have been defined and seem to have met with almost universal acceptance among professional students of international affairs as well as the lay public. Debate—when it is not stifled by the pressures of nationalism and patriotism—is mainly confined to technical questions of how best to attain the goals of existing policy. And this unanimity has been achieved without the necessity of putting a single person under police detention or arrest.

Pluralism and Public Opinion

The most reliable defense that a free society has against the tyranny of public opinion is the fragmentation of power that has already been identified as its definitive characteristic. This pluralism serves as a barrier against the excesses of both government propaganda and official secrecy, and its role is essential in both respects, for the influence of government upon public opinion rests equally upon its capacity to disseminate and to withhold information. The existence of competing centers of power within society serves to guarantee that official pronouncements will not go uncontested, if there is any question of their accuracy on matters of fact or interpretation, and it insures that efforts to conceal information will be subject to frequent challenge.

In American as in other democratic societies this pluralism is partly reflected by a widespread distribution of status and influence among various parts of the population. This dispersion of power has been maintained in spite of the very substantial breakdown that has occurred in sectional and local loyalties, for the decline in the importance of geographic factors as a source of diversity has been very largely offset by the development of new alignments based on economic rather than regional loyalties. Today, it is the tie of occupation, whether in business, labor, or agriculture, that serves to differentiate'society into discrete segments, each capable of resisting indoctrination by virtue of its ability to challenge government propaganda regarding matters which affect its own economic welfare with facts and interpretations that may well be at variance with official pronouncements.

Beyond this diversification of the community which itself serves as an important check upon efforts to mold opinion on a national scale, there are groups which have taken direct action in an effort to curb governmental abuse of its control over information. Certainly no segment of society has exercised a more important influence in this respect than the editors, publishers, commentators, and working reporters whose main occupation is the reporting of public affairs. The journalistic profession as a whole has a very tangible self-interest in preventing capricious use of the governmental power to release or suppress news about current events, since the press itself makes a living off the news.

To be sure, the claims this group makes for access to information are at times so sweeping as to be unreasonable. Even apart from security considerations, the case for retaining some measure of privacy in the conduct of governmental affairs is, as already suggested, a strong one, whether such privacy is designed to stimulate candor on the part of officials participating in executive deliberations or to shield the affairs of private citizens from needless public exposure. (Certainly the most famous of all resorts to privacy occurred in the framing of the Constitution itself.) But privacy generally is a right that finds little esteem in the practice of American democracy, and it certainly merits more respect than it usually receives from the newspaper community.[6]

Still, it is far better to have a press which is independent enough to carry on a vigorous fight against government secrecy, or as the case may be, propaganda on the part of executive officials, than to have a newspaper industry which leans entirely upon official handouts for the information it carries on governmental affairs, and refrains from all news-gathering activity which might deprive it of official favor. A press which errs on the side of aggressive zeal is infinitely to be preferred to one which errs on the side of timidity. This zeal is doubly necessary in areas like foreign affairs, where the factors of apathy and nationalism conspire to give official information a sanctity and credibility it lacks in most other areas of public discussion.

The balance of power within society is not the only check upon official power to control information, for the machinery of American government itself is structured to achieve this same objective. The existence of an independent judiciary and of a legislature with broad powers of inquiry internalizes restraints upon excesses in the field of secrecy and publicity within the framework of government itself. The important role that the judiciary plays in curbing executive efforts to conceal information when such concealment might adversely affect the rights of private citizens engaged in litigation has already been commented on.

With respect to the legislature, it may fairly be said that Congress is beyond question the strongest check we have upon executive abuse of the power to control information. No institution other than a legislative body has the authority, the legitimacy, or the sanctions to enforce disclosure and to discourage propaganda on the part of executive officials. Without the right of appeal which journalists now have to the leg-

---

[6] See, in this respect, the discussion on pp. 103–105.

islature, it is doubtful if newsmen themselves would enjoy nearly as much success as they do in policing executive practices in the field of information.

At the same time, however, Congress has not always made effective use of its power in this area. The extent to which the legislature has itself contributed to the development of excessive secrecy, particularly in the area intersected by science and national defense, has already been charted.[7] As one observer testifying before Congress noted:

> . . . Congress has its own responsibility in the creation of an atmosphere in which secrecy has been so heavily promoted during the past decade . . . a statement from Congress, making it clear that there was a change in climate in Congress' approach to this issue, would go far, I think, toward encouraging our civil servants and public officials to act more bravely with respect to their responsibilities when they are confronted with security questions.[8]

The most vigorous step Congress has taken to check the growth of executive secrecy was the establishment of the Moss Subcommittee on Government Information in 1955. Even apart from the specific investigations undertaken by the committee, its very presence in the scheme of things has undoubtedly been of substantial importance in deterring secretive practices that might otherwise have occurred. While the committee has, on several occasions, blown up cases involving the withholding of information far out of proportion to their real significance, it has nonetheless served the very useful purpose of giving continuity to the task of legislative oversight of executive information practices—a function which the legislature otherwise performs only on an *ad hoc* basis as cases involving the withholding of information come to the atten-

[7] See Chap. 3, especially pp. 47–51.
[8] See *Hearings*, House Subcommittee on Government Information, 84th Cong., 2d sess., March 7, 8, and 9, 1956, p. 919.

tion of individual legislators or committees.[9] The activities of a committee of this kind also represent a more effective way of singling out undesirable practices of secrecy than the passage of general statutes requiring disclosure. As already noted, such laws must necessarily be couched in ambiguous language and leave ample room for the exceptional cases in which secrecy is to be permitted.

This committee might also assume greater responsibility for exercising surveillance over executive needs and policies in the field of publicity as well as secrecy. The subject of "managing the news"—as James Reston termed it [10]—has been comparatively neglected during the past decade as legislative attention has been centered on executive efforts to conceal information. The principal difficulty which has obstructed adequate legislative review of executive efforts to manipulate opinion through the release of information is that a great deal of this activity has occurred in the area of defense and foreign affairs, and it has had the objective of furthering national interests in the cold war with the Soviet Union.

As a result, any thorough inquiry into cold war propaganda that this government may be disseminating to its own population could easily be construed as giving aid and comfort to the enemy. The gingerly care with which the U-2 incident was handled by Congress suggests the caution with which legislative oversight of administration is carried on when the legislature feels that one false step on its part may bring down the charge that it is imperiling the national security. Bureaucratic head-hunting is a much more dangerous pastime for a congressman when it is carried on in the CIA than when

[9] A five-year summary of the cases investigated by the committee may be found in *Twenty-Fourth Report by the Committee on Government Operations*, 86th Cong., 2d sess., House Report No. 2084, July 2, 1960, pp. 4-35.
[10] See *Hearings*, House Subcommittee on Government Information, 84th Cong., 1st sess., Nov. 7, 1955, p. 25. See also the discussion of "managed news" in Herbert Brucker, *Freedom of Information* (N.Y., 1949), pp. 99-108.

it is conducted in the much safer precincts of domestic agencies.

There is one other aspect of the American governmental system which displays the pluralism by which executive control over information is primarily limited. This is the factor of vigorous competition within the cadres of bureaucracy—a competition which spills over and manifests itself in the form of public exposure by one agency of suppression or distortion of information in which another agency is alleged to be engaged. This phenomenon has already been commented on in connection with earlier discussion of leaks by executive agencies.[11] During the period since World War II, conflict among executive agencies has played a very important role in bringing into public view erroneous claims or secret embarrassments on the part of one or another of the armed forces. Typical of this practice was the implication of Navy officials in the preparation of a document in 1949 which depreciated the claims which had been made for the Air Force's B-36 super bomber. This was after the Navy had been denied the right to construct a giant carrier through which it would have attained its own capability in the heavy bomber field.[12] This kind of infighting within bureaucracy makes it much more difficult for agencies to engage in deceptive practices in the field of secrecy or publicity.

Secrecy and Security

The most difficult question faced by any democratic society today with respect to the relationship between government and public opinion is the degree to which considerations of national security justify executive officials in withholding in-

[11] See pp. 78–79, 200.
[12] See *New York Times*, Aug. 27, 1949, p. 6.

formation from the public. For while it is often assumed that administrators are on the firmest of all grounds in refusing to disclose information in the area of defense and foreign affairs, the truth of the matter is that the impact of secrecy upon national security presents democratic society with some of its gravest dilemmas. This is a fact that needs to be underlined before concluding any discussion of publicity and secrecy in the operations of the modern democratic state.

It is commonly assumed, for example, that nations always advance their security by keeping information on the possession and development of new weapons secret. This is not actually the case. Nations have sometimes found it highly advantageous to give the maximum of publicity to the capability of their weapons. This is why fleets of naval vessels and squadrons of military aircraft have been sent on trips to far corners of the world as demonstrations of strength. And at the present time the publicity the Russians have given to their achievements in space, as well as the fanfare which has accompanied the development of the Polaris submarine by the United States, provide excellent illustrations of the pursuit of security through publicity.

A scientific observer has suggested that on at least one occasion a failure to give adequate publicity to an achievement in weapons technology had disastrous consequences for this nation's military position:

> In the case of radar, secrecy seriously delayed its development, and neither technical nor tactical progress was very appreciable. As a consequence, although it was technically and demonstrably adequate to have done this relatively simple job, radar failed to prevent Pearl Harbor (a tactical failure born of military ignorance imposed by secrecy, for the clear warning of radar was ignored.) Had they known our radar protection of Pearl Harbor, there is at least a reasonable doubt that the Japanese would have attempted a surprise.

In any event, our own commanders would not have been ignorant of the powerful tools at their command, and the outcome might well have been very different.

Moreover, the development of airborne radar applications awaited the war, for at its commencement we had no antisubmarine radar, no night fighters, no means for extensive air search. The absence of such weapons is directly attributable to the technological ignorance and delays resulting from secrecy.

Had airborne radar been developed and advertised openly, the consequent great progress in these developments might have so weakened the German confidence in their submarine supremacy, or in their capabilities for strategic air attack, that the war might not have occurred.

In any event, our shipping losses after its beginning would certainly have been less than the tragic millions of tons.[13]

What this illustration suggests is that weapons designed to protect a nation from surprise attack do not achieve their maximum effect in providing security if their existence is unknown to a potential aggressor. It also calls attention to two other respects in which (as has already been noted in earlier discussion) excessive secrecy may have a detrimental effect upon national security. One is the way in which secrecy may slow up the rate of scientific development upon which continuing security depends by hindering communications among scientists.[14] The other stems from the "need to know" criterion which restricts the circulation of classified information to very limited groups of officials. In many cases the application of this principle handicaps key officials in discharging their responsibilities because it leaves them ignorant of facts on which

---

[13] See *Hearings*, House Subcommittee on Government Information, 84th Cong., 2d sess., March 7, 8, and 9, 1956, p. 757. The security value of disclosure is discussed by Bernard Brodie, "Military Demonstration and Disclosure of New Weapons," *World Politics*, Vol. V (April, 1953), pp. 281–301.

[14] See pp. 30–31.

policy should be based. In a discussion of science and government at Harvard University, C. P. Snow argued that World War II might have ended sooner, and with less cost, if "secret politics" in Great Britain had not affected the conduct of the war.[15]

Former Atomic Energy Commissioner Thomas E. Murray has provided us with an astounding example of the lengths to which the "need to know" principle may be carried. He writes that in 1957 "I wished to convey certain factual information about the composition of our nuclear stockpile to certain members of the National Security Council, including the Secretary of State. It was ruled by the AEC that they had no 'need to know' the facts I wished to present." [16] The closeness with which the AEC thus guards classified data on atomic energy has also been an obstacle to civil defense efforts in this country.

Taken together, these arguments provide impressive testimony to the fact that an effective national defense depends as much upon adequate publicity regarding a nation's weaponry as it does upon keeping military secrets safe from disclosure. At least a minimum measure of publicity on defense matters is indispensable for informing scientists and public officials about weapons with which they should be familiar. And on many questions, it may be highly useful to bring much broader circles of the public within the framework of knowledgeable discussion. As one leading scientific authority has written:

[15] Baltimore M rning Sun, Dec. 1, 1960, p. 9. In an article published shortly after his appearance at Harvard, Snow also asserted that the critical decisions made in secret during World War II were "made or indorsed by men— presidents, prime ministers, cabinet members, military leaders—who were not able to comprehend in depth the scientific arguments for and against the decisions." "Whether We Live or Die," Life, Vol. 50 (Feb. 3, 1961), pp. 90–104. See also by Snow, Science and Government (Cambridge, 1961).

[16] Thomas E. Murray, Nuclear Policy for War and Peace (Cleveland, 1960), p. 213. See also John G. Palfrey, "The Problem of Secrecy," in "The Impact of Atomic Energy," Annals of the American Academy of Political and Social Science, Vol. 290 (Nov., 1953), pp. 94–95.

Our government cannot act strongly without ample support from public opinion. For wise action, an informed public opinion is necessary. When secrecy intervenes, an informed public opinion can hardly exist. Too often we have, instead, a manipulated public opinion formed by leaks, half-truths, innuendoes, and sometimes by outright distortion of the actual facts.[17]

The side-effects which flow from an ill-informed public opinion may be even more serious:

. . . the need to protect "the secret" has contributed to a jittery climate of public opinion—at least among some influential publics—that seems to foster suspicion, distrust, fear of heterodoxy, support for a variety of measures of public and private repression, and the enhancement of the power of leaders who manipulate these sentiments.[18]

To be sure, the number of private citizens who are alert to any particular issue of public affairs in a democracy may be small as compared to the total population, but the contribution such an attentive group can make to the development of public policy may be of critical importance.

But even beyond the fact that the practice of withholding information can be a liability as well as an asset to national security, any appraisal of the role of secrecy in a free society must also consider that even where such secrecy does actually serve to advance national security, this fact alone does not always establish its desirability in the operations of a democratic state. Since democratic communities exist to serve other values besides national security, the extent to which the practice of withholding information furthers security interests must always be measured against the possibility that it may at

[17] I. I. Rabi, "The Cost of Secrecy," *The Atlantic*, Vol. 206 (August, 1960), p. 41.
[18] Robert A. Dahl, "Atomic Energy and the Democratic Process," in "The Impact of Atomic Energy," *Annals* of the American Academy of Political and Social Science, Vol. 290 (November, 1953), p. 2.

the same time exact so high a price in terms of other values which are equally central to the well-being of a democratic community that it simply cannot be justified.

It is quite clear, for example, that insofar as secrecy in government seriously impedes the free flow of communications among citizens, it constitutes a real threat to the informed public discussion that is at the core of democracy. Where this occurs, it is not at all certain that a community should not choose, from the point of view of its own value system, to tolerate some measure of insecurity in order to gain access to information it needs in order to exercise influence over decisions on vital matters of public policy.[19] This choice takes on increased rationality today from the fact that the net of secrecy has been thrown around so wide a span of scientific and technical data, far broader in scope than was the case in the day when nations had only to conceal a few matters of a purely military nature. A situation has been created in modern democracy in which governmental decisions affecting entire populations are made by a few individuals operating on the basis of information with which they, and they alone, are familiar.[20]

In the end, therefore, there is no simple way of reconciling the conflicting claims of publicity, secrecy, and democracy. In this area as elsewhere, no democratic community can escape the difficult task of choosing among alternative means of attaining agreed upon values, or the even harder necessity of foregoing one goal if it is to attain another. Even in the

[19] For a discussion of the tendency to give security an exclusive as well as a pre-eminent place in democratic society, see Arnold Wolfers, "National Security as an Ambiguous Symbol," *Political Science Quarterly*, Vol. LXVII (December, 1952), pp. 481–502.

[20] As Robert A. Dahl has put it: "The institutionalization of secrecy has concentrated, in the hands of a few people, control over decisions of a great magnitude for the values of a larger number of persons than in all probability were ever affected by any old-fashioned authoritarian leader." *Op. cit.*, pp. 2–3.

pursuit of security, great care must be taken lest information procedures that are designed to strengthen the nation actually endanger its safety, or alternatively, so weaken the process of public discussion as to impoverish the vitality of democracy itself. One thing is certain. No community which is apathetic about the problems discussed in these pages will come close to striking a reasonable balance between secrecy and publicity in the operations of government. It will oscillate, as American society often does, between the extremes of secrecy and publicity, in response to sporadic fears and crises that stir it from its customary slumber.

INDEX